THE ROSE OF TIME
New and Selected Poems

時間的玫瑰

Also by Bei Dao

POETRY

At the Sky's Edge: Poems 1991–1996
The August Sleepwalker
Forms of Distance
Old Snow
Unlock

SHORT STORIES

Waves

ESSAYS

Blue House
Midnight's Gate

THE ROSE OF TIME
New and Selected Poems

Bei Dao

Edited by Eliot Weinberger

TRANSLATED BY *Yanbing Chen, David Hinton, Chen Maiping,
Iona Man-Cheong, Bonnie S. McDougall, and Eliot Weinberger*

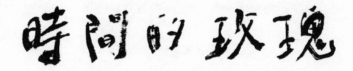

A New Directions Book

Interior design by Eileen Baumgartner
Chinese calligraphy by Ouyang Jianghe

Manufactured in the United States of America
New Directions Books are printed on acid-free paper.
First published as a New Directions Paperbook (NDP1160) in 2009
Published simultaneously in Canada by Penguin Books Canada Limited

Library of Congress Cataloging-in-Publication Data

Beidao, 1949–
    [Poems. English & Chinese. Selections]
    The rose of time / Bei Dao; edited by Eliot Weinberger; translated by
Yanbing Chen ... [et al.].
        p. cm. -- (New Directions paperbook; 1160)
    Includes index.
    ISBN 978-0-8112-1848-1 (pbk. : acid-free paper)
1. Beidao, 1949---Translations into English. I. Weinberger, Eliot. II. Chen,
Yanbing. III. Title.
    PL2892.E525A2 2009
    895.1'152--dc22
                                                        2009035682

New Directions Books are published for James Laughlin
by New Directions Publishing Corporation
80 Eighth Avenue, New York, NY 10011

For Qi, Tiantian, and Dodo

CONTENTS

from FORMS OF DISTANCE (1994)
translated by David Hinton

from LANDSCAPE OVER ZERO (1996)
translated by David Hinton and Yanbing Chen

from UNLOCK (2000)
translated by Eliot Weinberger and Iona Man-Cheong

THE ROSE OF TIME: NEW POEMS
translated by Eliot Weinberger

It has been forty years since I started writing poetry at the age of twenty, when I was a construction worker at a site in the mountains more than two hundred miles from Beijing. I would have been shocked if I had been able to see what would happen later on—it is unimaginable, and I might have been proud of myself. But when I look back at that moment, trying to trace the origins, my feelings are complicated and perplexed: How did this writing happen? Where does the primal driving force come from? Does so-called fate lead to writing, or writing lead to fate? How far can poetry go beyond the limits on the road of language? Is there anything a poet can do when it seems human imagination itself has been getting paler day by day in our time?

I was born in 1949 in Beijing. As Chairman Mao declared the birth of the Peoples' Republic of China from the rostrum in Tiananmen Square, I was lying in my cradle no more than a thousand yards away. My fate seems to have been intertwined with that of China ever since. I received a privileged, but brief, education. I was a student at the best high school in Beijing, until the Cultural Revolution broke out in 1966. All the schools were closed, and three years later I was assigned to work in the state-run construction industry. I worked as a concrete mixer for five years, and then another six years as a blacksmith. This experience of hard labor, living at the bottom of society, eventually helped me a great deal. It broadened my understanding of life in a way that was tangible and material, something that books could hardly be capable of achieving.

It was under those harsh circumstances of life that I began my creative writing. I finished the first draft of a novella, *Waves*, in a darkroom, while supposedly developing photos for a propaganda exhibition about the construction site. That was one of the grimmest periods of contemporary China, when reading and writing were forbidden games. But underground creative writing was breaking through the frozen shell of the earth.

On December 23, 1978, I, together with some friends, launched the first non-official literary journal in China since 1949, *Today*. The "misty" or "obscure" poetry—a pejorative term applied by the authorities—that appeared in *Today* was able to challenge the dominance of the official social discourse by opening a new space, new possibilities for the Chinese language. Inevitably, the journal was banned after two years of its existence, but it began a new phase in the history of Chinese literature.

Berlin in 1989 marked the beginning of my life in exile. For the next four years, I lived in six countries in Europe. *Today* was revived in 1990, and has continued to be published abroad ever since. It remains the only Chinese avant-garde literary journal whose existence transcends geographic boundaries. As its chief editor, I have been engaged, alongside writers within China, in a long-term literary resistance—not only to the hegemony of the official discourse, but also to the degree of commercialization throughout the world. A once-mimeographed journal floating across the oceans has managed to survive in environments where other languages are spoken.

In truth, I am not quite confident about my writing when I look back. It reminds me of those days of blacksmithing, when I was frustrated by the iron works I had made. I realize that a poet and a blacksmith are much alike: both of them chase after a perfect dream that is unrealizable. I once, in an early poem, wrote the lines: "freedom is nothing but the distance / between the hunter and the hunted." It is the predicament, as well, of writing poetry: when you are hunting poetry, it turns out that you are hunted by poetry. In this sense, you are both hunter and hunted, but poetry is the distance like freedom.

BEI DAO

THE ROSE of TIME
New and Selected Poems

時間的玫瑰

from THE AUGUST SLEEPWALKER (1972–1986)
translated by Bonnie S. McDougall

太阳城札记

生 命
太阳也上升了

爱 情
恬静。雁群飞过
荒芜的处女地
老树倒下了，嘎然一声
空中飘落着咸涩的雨

自 由
飘
撕碎的纸屑

孩 子
容纳整个海洋的图画
叠成了一只白鹤

姑 娘
颤动的虹
采集飞鸟的花翎

青 春
红波浪
浸透孤独的桨

艺 术
亿万个辉煌的太阳
显现在打碎的镜子上

人 民
月亮被撕成闪耀的麦粒
播在诚实的天空和土地

劳 动
手，围拢地球

Life
The sun has risen too

Love
Tranquillity. The wild geese have flown
over the virgin wasteland
the old tree has toppled with a crash
acrid salty rain drifts through the air

Freedom
Torn scraps of paper
fluttering

Child
A picture enclosing the whole ocean
folds into a white crane

Girl
A shimmering rainbow
gathers brightly colored feathers

Youth
Red waves
drown a solitary oar

Art
A million scintillating suns
appear in the shattered mirror

People
The moon is torn into gleaming grains of wheat
and sown in the honest sky and earth

Labor
Hands, encircling the earth

命 运
孩子随意敲打着栏杆
栏杆随意敲打着夜晚

信 仰
羊群溢出绿色的洼地
牧童吹起单调的短笛

和 平
在帝王死去的地方
那枝老枪抽枝、发芽
成了残废者的拐杖

祖 国
她被铸在青铜的盾牌上
靠着博物馆发黑的板墙

生 活
网

4

Fate
The child strikes the railing at random
at random the railing strikes the night

Faith
A flock of sheep spills out of the green ditch
the shepherd boy plays his monotonous pipe

Peace
In the land where the king is dead
the old rifle sprouting branches and buds
has become a cripple's cane

Motherland
Cast on a shield of bronze
she leans against a blackened museum wall

Living
A net

回 答

卑鄙是卑鄙者的通行证，
高尚是高尚者的墓志铭，
看吧，在那镀金的天空中，
飘满了死者弯曲的倒影。

冰川纪过去了，
为什么到处都是冰凌？
好望角发现了，
为什么死海里千帆相竞？

我来到这个世界上，
只带着纸、绳索和身影，
为了在审判之前，
宣读那被判决了的声音：

告诉你吧，世界
我——不——相——信！
纵使你脚下有一千名挑战者，
那就把我算作第一千零一名。

我不相信天是蓝的，
我不相信雷的回声，
我不相信梦是假的，
我不相信死无报应。

如果海洋注定要决堤，
就让所有的苦水都注入我心中，
如果陆地注定要上升，
就让人类重新选择生存的峰顶。

新的转机和闪闪星斗，
正在缀满没有遮拦的天空，
那是五千年的象形文字，
那是未来人们凝视的眼睛。

THE ANSWER

Debasement is the password of the base,
Nobility the epitaph of the noble.
See how the gilded sky is covered
With the drifting twisted shadows of the dead.

The Ice Age is over now,
Why is there ice everywhere?
The Cape of Good Hope has been discovered,
Why do a thousand sails contest the Dead Sea?

I came into this world
Bringing only paper, rope, a shadow.
To proclaim before the judgment
The voice that has been judged:

Let me tell you, world.
I—do—not—believe!
If a thousand challengers lie beneath your feet,
Count me as number one thousand and one.

I don't believe the sky is blue;
I don't believe in thunder's echoes;
I don't believe that dreams are false;
I don't believe that death has no revenge.

If the sea is destined to breach the dikes
Let all the brackish water pour into my heart;
If the land is destined to rise
Let humanity choose a peak for existence again.

A new conjunction and glimmering stars
Adorn the unobstructed sky now:
They are the pictographs from five thousand years.
They are the watchful eyes of future generations.

走 吧
　　　——给L

走吧，
落叶吹进深谷，
歌声却没有归宿。

走吧
冰上的月光，
已从河床上溢出。

走吧，
眼睛望着同一块天空，
心敲击着暮色的鼓。

走吧，
我们没有失去记忆，
我们去寻找生命的湖。

走吧，
路呵路，
飘满了红罂粟。

LET'S GO
        for L

Let's go—
Fallen leaves blow into deep valleys
But the song has no home to return to.

Let's go—
Moonlight on the ice
Has spilled beyond the river bed.

Let's go—
Eyes gaze at the same patch of sky
Hearts strike the twilight drum.

Let's go—
We have not lost our memories
We shall search for life's pool.

Let's go—
The road, the road
Is covered with a drift of scarlet poppies.

一束

在我和世界之间
你是海湾，是帆
是缆绳忠实的两端
你是喷泉，是风
是童年清脆的呼喊

在我和世界之间
你是画框，是窗口
是开满野花的田园
你是呼吸，是床头
是陪伴星星的夜晚

在我和世界之间
你是日历，是罗盘
是暗中滑行的光线
你是履历，是书签
是写在最后的序言

在我和世界之间
你是纱幕，是雾
是映入梦中的灯盏
你是口笛，是无言之歌
是石雕低垂的眼帘

在我和世界之间
你是鸿沟，是池沼
是正在下陷的深渊
你是栅栏，是墙垣
是盾牌上永久的图案

A BOUQUET

Between me and the world
You are a bay, a sail
The faithful ends of a rope
You are a fountain, a wind
A shrill childhood cry

Between me and the world
You are a picture frame, a window
A field covered with wild flowers
You are a breath, a bed
A night that keeps the stars company

Between me and the world
You are a calendar, a compass
A ray of light that slips through the gloom
You are a biographical sketch, a bookmark
A preface that comes at the end

Between me and the world
You are a gauze curtain, a mist
A lamp shining into my dreams
You are a bamboo flute, a song without words
A closed eyelid carved in stone

Between me and the world
You are a chasm, a pool
An abyss plunging down
You are a balustrade, a wall
A shield's eternal pattern

睡吧，山谷

睡吧，山谷
快用蓝色的云雾蒙住天空
蒙住野百合苍白的眼睛
睡吧，山谷
快用雨的脚步去追逐风
追逐布谷鸟不安的啼鸣

睡吧，山谷
我们躲在这里
仿佛躲进一个千年的梦中
时间不再从草叶上滑过
太阳的钟摆停在云层后面
不再摇落晚霞和黎明

旋转的树林
甩下无数颗坚硬的松果
护卫着两行脚印
我们的童年和季节一起
走过那条弯弯曲曲的小路
花粉沾满了荆丛

呵，多么寂静
抛出去的石子没有回声
也许，你在探求什么
——从心到心
一道彩虹正悄然升起
——从眼睛到眼睛

睡吧，山谷
睡吧，风
山谷睡在蓝色的云雾里
风，睡在我们手掌中

SLEEP, VALLEY

Sleep, valley
with blue mist quickly cover the sky
and the wild lilies' pale eyes
Sleep, valley
with rainsteps quickly chase away the wind
and the anxious cries of the cuckoo

Sleep, valley
here we hide
as if in a thousand-year dream
time no longer glides past blades of grass
stopped behind layers of clouds, the sun's clock
no longer swings down evening glow or dawn

Spinning trees
toss down countless hard pine cones
protecting two lines of footprints
our childhoods walked with the seasons
along this winding path
and pollen drenched the brambles

Ah, it's so quiet and still
the cast stone has no echo
perhaps you are searching for something
—from heart to heart
a rainbow rises in silence
—from eye to eye

Sleep, valley
sleep, wind
valley, asleep in blue mist
wind, asleep in our hands

船 票

他没有船票
又怎能登上甲板
铁锚的链条哗哗作响
也惊动这里的夜晚

海啊,海
退潮中上升的岛屿
和心一样孤单
没有灌木丛柔和的影子
没有炊烟
划出闪电的船桅
又被闪电击成了碎片
无数次风暴
在坚硬的鱼鳞和贝壳上
在水母小小的伞上
留下了静止的图案
一个古老的故事
在浪花与浪花之间相传

他没有船票

海啊,海
密集在礁石上的苔藓
向赤裸的午夜蔓延
顺着鸥群暗中发光的羽毛
依附在月亮表面
潮水沉寂了
海螺和美人鱼开始歌唱

他没有船票

岁月并没有从此中断
沉船正生火待发
重新点燃了红珊瑚的火焰
当浪峰耸起
死者的眼睛闪烁不定
从海洋深处浮现

BOAT TICKET

He doesn't have a boat ticket
how can he go on board
the clanking of the anchor chain
disturbs the night here

the sea, the sea
the island that rises from the ebbing tide
as lonely as a heart
lacks the soft shadows of bushes
and chimney smoke
the mast that flashes lightning
is struck into fragments by lightning
innumerable storms
have left behind fixed patterns
on rigid scales and shells
and the small umbrellas of jellyfish
an ancient tale
is handed on by the ocean spray from wave to wave

he doesn't have a boat ticket

the sea, the sea
the lichen tightly massed on the reef
spreads toward the naked midnight
along the seagulls' feathers gleaming in the dark
and clings to the surface of the moon
the tide has fallen silent
conch and mermaid begin to sing

he doesn't have a boat ticket

time hasn't come to a stop
in the sunken boat the fire is being stoked
rekindling red coral flames
when the waves tower up
glittering indeterminately, the eyes of the dead
float up from the ocean depths

他没有船票

是啊，令人晕眩
那片晾在沙滩上的阳光
多么令人晕眩

他没有船票

he doesn't have a boat ticket

yes, it makes you dizzy
the sunlight drying out on the beach
makes you so terribly dizzy

he doesn't have a boat ticket

无 题

把手伸给我
让我那肩头挡住的世界
不再打扰你
假如爱不是遗忘的话
苦难也不是记忆
记住我的话吧
一切都不会过去
即使只有最后一棵白杨树
像没有铭刻的墓碑
在路的尽头耸立
落叶也会说话
在翻滚中褪色、变白
慢慢地冻结起来
托起我们深深的足迹
当然，谁也不知道明天
明天从另一个早晨开始
那时我们将沉沉睡去

UNTITLED

Stretch out your hands to me
don't let the world blocked by my shoulder
disturb you any longer
if love is not forgotten
hardship leaves no memory
remember what I say
not everything will pass
if there is only one last aspen
standing tall at the end of the road
like a gravestone without an epitaph
the falling leaves will also speak
fading paling as they tumble
slowly they freeze over
holding our heavy footprints
of course, no one knows tomorrow
tomorrow begins from another dawn
when we will be fast asleep

宣 告
　　——献给遇罗克

也许最后的时刻到了
我没有留下遗嘱
只留下笔，给我的母亲
我并不是英雄
在没有英雄的年代里
我只想做一个人

宁静的地平线
分开了生者和死者的行列
我只能选择天空
决不跪在地上
以显出刽子手们的高大
好阻挡那自由的风

从星星的弹孔里
将流出血红的黎明

DECLARATION
for Yu Luoke

Perhaps the final hour is come
I have left no testament
Only a pen, for my mother
I am no hero
In an age without heroes
I just want to be a man

The still horizon
Divides the ranks of the living and the dead
I can only choose the sky
I will not kneel on the ground
Allowing the executioners to look tall
The better to obstruct the wind of freedom

From star-like bullet holes shall flow
A blood-red dawn

结局或开始
　　——献给遇罗克

我，站在这里
代替另一个被杀害的人
为了每当太阳升起
让沉重的影子像道路
穿过整个国土

悲哀的雾
覆盖着补丁般错落的屋顶
在房子与房子之间
烟囱喷吐着灰烬般的人群
温暖从明亮的树梢吹散
逗留在贫困的烟头上
一只只疲倦的手中
升起低沉的乌云

以太阳的名义
黑暗在公开地掠夺
沉默依然是东方的故事
人民在古老的壁画上
默默地永生
默默地死去

呵，我的土地
你为什么不再歌唱
难道连黄河纤夫的绳索
也像绷断的琴弦
不再发出鸣响
难道时间这面晦暗的镜子
也永远背对着你
只留下星星和浮云

我寻找着你
在一次次梦中
一个个多雾的夜里或早晨
我寻找春天和苹果树
蜜蜂牵动的一缕缕微风

AN END OR A BEGINNING
for Yu Luoke

Here I stand
Replacing another, who has been murdered
So that each time the sun rises
A heavy shadow, like a road
Shall run across the land

A sorrowing mist
Covers the uneven patchwork of roofs
Between one house and another
Chimneys spout ashy crowds
Warmth effuses from gleaming trees
Lingering on the wretched cigarette stubs
Low black clouds arise
From every tired hand

In the name of the sun
Darkness plunders openly
Silence is still the story of the East
People on age-old frescoes
Silently live forever
Silently die and are gone

Ah, my beloved land
Why don't you sing anymore
Can it be true that even the ropes of the Yellow River towmen
Like sundered lute-strings
Reverberate no more
True that time, this dark mirror
Has also turned its back on you forever
Leaving only stars and drifting clouds behind

I look for you
In every dream
Every foggy night or morning
I look for spring and apple trees
Every wisp of breeze stirred up by honey bees

我寻找海岸的潮汐
浪峰上的阳光变成的鸥群
我寻找砌在墙里的传说
你和我被遗忘的姓名

如果鲜血会使你肥沃
明天的枝头上
成熟的果实
会留下我的颜色

必须承认
在死亡白色的寒光中
我，战栗了
谁愿意做陨石
或受难者冰冷的塑像
看着不熄的青春之火
在别人的手中传递
即使鸽子落到肩上
也感不到体温和呼吸
它们梳理一番羽毛
又匆匆飞去

我是人
我需要爱
我渴望在情人的眼睛里
度过每个宁静的黄昏
在摇篮的晃动中
等待着儿子第一声呼唤
在草地和落叶上
在每一道真挚的目光上
我写下生活的诗
这普普通通的愿望
如今成了做人的全部代价

一生中
我曾多次撒谎
却始终诚实地遵守着

I look for the seashore's ebb and flow
The seagulls formed from sunlight on the waves
I look for the stories built into the wall
Your forgotten name and mine

If fresh blood could make you fertile
The ripened fruit
On tomorrow's branches
Would bear my color

I must admit
That I trembled
In the death-white chilly light
Who wants to be a meteorite
Or a martyr's ice-cold statue
Watching the unextinguished fire of youth
Pass into another's hand
Even if doves alight on its shoulder
It can't feel their bodies' warmth and breath
They preen their wings
And quickly fly away

I am a man
I need love
I long to pass each tranquil dusk
Under my love's eyes
Waiting in the cradle's rocking
For the child's first cry
On the grass and fallen leaves
On every sincere gaze
I write poems of life
This universal longing
Has now become the whole cost of being a man

I have lied many times
In my life
But I have always honestly kept to

一个儿时的诺言
因此，那与孩子的心
不能相容的世界
再也没有饶恕过我

我，站在这里
代替另一个被杀害的人
没有别的选择
在我倒下的地方
将会有另一个人站起
我的肩上是风
风上是闪烁的星群

也许有一天
太阳变成了萎缩的花环
垂放在
每一个不屈的战士
森林般生长的墓碑前
乌鸦，这夜的碎片
纷纷扬扬

The promise I made as a child
So that the world which cannot tolerate
A child's heart
Has still not forgiven me

Here I stand
Replacing another, who has been murdered
I have no other choice
And where I fall
Another will stand
A wind rests on my shoulders
Stars glimmer in the wind

Perhaps one day
The sun will become a withered wreath
To hang before
The growing forest of gravestones
Of each unsubmitting fighter
Black crows the night's tatters
Flock thick around

AUTHOR'S NOTE: *The first draft of this poem was written in 1975. Some good friends of mine fought side by side with Yu Luoke, and two of them were thrown into prison where they languished for three years. This poem records our tragic and indignant protest in that tragic and indignant period.*

港口的梦

当月光层层涌入港口
这夜色仿佛透明
一级级磨损的石阶
通向天空
通向我的梦境

我回到了故乡
给母亲带回珊瑚和盐
珊瑚长成林木
盐，融化了冰层
姑娘们的睫毛
抖落下成熟的麦粒
峭壁衰老的额头
吹过湿润的风
我的情歌
到每扇窗户里去做客
酒的泡沫溢到街上
变成一盏盏路灯
我走向霞光照临的天际
转过身来
深深地鞠了一躬

浪花洗刷着甲板和天空
星星在罗盘上
找寻自己白昼的方位
是的，我不是水手
生来就不是水手
但我把心挂在船舷
像锚一样
和伙伴们出航

HARBOR DREAMS

When moonlight pours into the harbor
the night air seems transparent
step by step the worn stone stairs
lead to the sky
lead to my dreams

I returned to my native town
bringing back coral and salt for my mother
the coral grew into a forest
the salt melted the ice
girls' quivering lashes
shed ripened grains of wheat
a moist wind blew
past the cliffs' decrepit foreheads
when my love song
paid a call at every window
beer foam spilled over the road
turning into a row of street lights
I walked toward the horizon glowing in the sunset
and turned around
to make a deep bow

The sea spray washed the deck and the sky
the stars searched for their daylight positions
on the compass
true, I'm not a sailor
not born to be a sailor
but I'll hang my heart on the side of the ship
like an anchor
and set sail with the crew

枫叶和七颗星星

世界小得像一条街的布景
我们相遇了，你点点头
省略了所有的往事
省略了问候
也许欢乐只是一个过程
一切都已经结束
可你为什么还戴着那块红头巾
看看吧，枫叶装饰的天空
多么晴朗，阳光
已移向最后一扇玻璃窗

巨大的屋顶后面
那七颗星星升起来
不再像一串成熟的葡萄
这是又一个秋天
当然，路灯就要亮了
我多想看看你的微笑
宽恕而冷漠
还有那平静的目光
路灯就要亮了

MAPLE LEAVES AND SEVEN STARS

The world is as small as a street scene
when we met you nodded briefly
dispensing with the past
and friendly greetings
happiness is just a passage perhaps
and all is at an end
but why do you still wear that red scarf
look, through the lace of maple leaves the sky
is very clear, and the sun
has shifted to the last windowpane

The seven stars ascending
behind the massive roofs
no longer look like a cluster of ripe grapes
it is another autumn
the street lights will soon be lit of course
I should dearly like to see your smile
forgiving but indifferent
and that calm gaze
the street lights will soon be lit

彗 星

回来，或永远走开
别这样站在门口
如同一尊石像
用并不期待回答的目光
谈论我们之间的一切

其实难以想象的
并不是黑暗，而是早晨
灯光将怎样延续下去
或许有彗星出现
拖曳着废墟中的瓦砾
和失败者的名字
让它们闪光、燃烧、化为灰烬

回来，我们重建家园
或永远走开，像彗星那样
灿烂而冷若冰霜
摈弃黑暗，又沉溺于黑暗中
穿过连接两个夜晚的白色走廊
在回声四起的山谷里
你独自歌唱

COMET

Come back or leave forever
don't stand like that at the door
like a statue made of stone
discussing everything between us
with a look that expects no answer

in fact what is hard to imagine
is not darkness but dawn
how long will the lamplight last
perhaps a comet may appear
trailing debris from the ruins
and a list of failures
letting them glitter, burn up, and turn into ash

come back, and we'll rebuild our home
or leave forever, like a comet
sparkling and cold like frost
discarding the dark, and sinking back into darkness again
going through the white corridor connecting two evenings
in the valley where echoes arise on all sides
you sing alone

归程

汽笛长鸣不已
难道你还想数清
那棵梧桐上的乌鸦
默默地记住我们
仿佛凭借这点点踪影
就不会迷失在另一场梦中

陈叶和红色的蓓蕾
在灌木丛上摇曳
其实并没有风
而藏匿于晨光中的霜
穿越车窗时
留下你苍白的倦容

是的，你不顾一切
总要踏上归程
昔日的短笛
在被抛弃的地方
早已经繁衍成树林
守望道路，廓清天空

THE WAY BACK

The whistle emits an interminable shriek
surely you don't want to keep counting
the crows on the wutong tree
silently memorizing them
as if these signs would prevent you
from losing your way in another dream

faded leaves and red buds
sway on the bushes
the wind has actually dropped
but passing by the carriage window
the frost congealed in the dawn light
leaves behind your pale and weary face

yes, in spite of everything
you still want to take the way back
in a place long abandoned
the bamboo pipes of the past
have multiplied into a forest
watching over the road
and sweeping the sky clean

履历

我曾正步走过广场
剃光脑袋
为了更好地寻找太阳
却在疯狂的季节里
转了向，隔着栅栏
会见那些表情冷漠的山羊
直到从盐碱地似的
白纸上看到理想
我弓起了脊背
自以为找到表达真理的
惟一方式，如同
烘烤着的鱼梦见海洋
万岁！我只他妈喊了一声
胡子就长出来了
纠缠着，像无数个世纪
我不得不和历史作战
并用刀子与偶像们
结成亲眷，到不是为了应付
那从蝇眼中分裂的世界
在争吵不休的书堆里
我们安然平分了
倒卖每一颗星星的小钱
一夜之间，我赌输了
腰带，又赤条条地回到世上
点着无声的烟卷
是给这午夜致命的一枪
当天地翻转过来
我被倒挂在
一棵墩布似的老树上
眺望

RÉSUMÉ

Once I goosestepped across the square
my head shaved bare
the better to seek the sun
but in that season of madness
seeing the cold-faced goats on the other side
of the fence I changed direction
when I saw my ideals
on blank paper like saline-alkaline soil
I bent my spine
believing I had found the only
way to express the truth, like
a baked fish dreaming of the sea
Long live . . . ! I shouted only once, damn it
then sprouted a beard
tangled like countless centuries
I was obliged to do battle with history
and at knifepoint formed a
family alliance with idols
not indeed to cope with
the world fragmented in a fly's eye
among piles of endlessly bickering books
calmly we divided into equal shares
the few coins we made from selling off each star
in a single night I gambled away
my belt, and returned naked again to the world
lighting a silent cigarette
it was a gun bringing death at midnight
when heaven and earth changed places
I hung upside down
on an old tree that looked like a mop
gazing into the distance

同谋

很多年过去了，云母
在泥沙里闪着光芒
又邪恶，又明亮
犹如蝮蛇眼睛中的太阳
手的丛林，一条条歧路出没
那只年轻的鹿在哪儿
或许只有墓地改变这里的
荒凉，组成了市镇
自由不过是
猎人与猎物之间的距离
当我们回头望去
在父辈们肖像的广阔背景上
蝙蝠划出的圆弧，和黄昏
一起消失

我们不是无辜的
早已和镜子中的历史成为
同谋，等待那一天
在火山岩浆里沉积下来
化作一股冷泉
重见黑暗

ACCOMPLICES

Many years have passed, mica
gleams in the mud
with a bright and evil light
like the sun in a viper's eyes
in a jungle of hands, roads branch off and disappear
where is the young deer
perhaps only a graveyard can change
this wilderness and assemble a town
freedom is nothing but the distance
between the hunter and the hunted
when we turn and look back
the arc drawn by bats
against the vast background of our fathers' portraits
fades with the dusk

we are not guiltless
long ago we became accomplices
of the history in the mirror, waiting for the day
to be deposited in lava
and turn into a cold spring
to meet the darkness once again

很多年

这是你，这是
被飞翔的阴影困扰的
你，忽明忽暗
我不再走向你
寒冷也让我失望
很多年，冰山形成以前
鱼曾浮出水面
沉下去，很多年
我小心翼翼
穿过缓缓流动的夜晚
灯火在钢叉上闪烁
很多年，寂寞
这没有钟的房间
离去的人也会带上
钥匙，很多年
在浓雾中吹起口哨
桥上的火车驶过
一个个季节
从田野的小车站出发
为每棵树逗留
开花结果，很多年

FOR MANY YEARS

This is you, this is
you, pressed upon by fleeting
shadows, now bright, now dark
no longer shall I go toward you
the cold also makes me despair
for many years, before the icebergs were formed
fish floated up to the water's surface
and sank down, for many years
stepping warily I
passed through the slowly drifting night
lamps glowed on the forked steel prongs
for many years, lonely is
the room without a clock
the people who left may also have taken
the key, for many years
the train on the bridge rushed past
whistling through the fog
season after season
set out from the small station among the fields
paused briefly for every tree
flowered and bore fruit, for many years

关于传统

野山羊站立在悬崖上
拱桥自建成之日
就已经衰老
在箭猪般丛生的年代里
谁又能看清地平线
日日夜夜，风铃
如文身的男人那样
阴沉，听不到祖先的语言
长夜默默地进入石头
搬动石头的愿望是
山，在历史课本中起伏

ON TRADITION

The mountain goat stands on the precipice
the arched bridge decrepit
from the day it was built
who can make out the horizon
through years as dense as porcupines
day and night, windchimes
as somber
as tattooed men, do not hear ancestral voices
the long night silently enters the stone
the wish to move the stone
is a mountain range rising and falling in history books

八月的梦游者

海底的石钟敲响
敲响，掀起了波浪

敲响的是八月
八月的正午没有太阳

涨满乳汁的三角帆
高耸在漂浮的尸体上

高耸的是八月
八月的苹果滚下山冈

熄灭已久的灯塔
被水手们的目光照亮

照亮的是八月
八月的集市又临霜降

海底的石钟敲响
敲响，掀起了波浪

八月的梦游者
看见过夜里的太阳

THE AUGUST SLEEPWALKER

the stone bell tolls on the seabed
its tolling stirs up the waves

it is august that tolls
there is no sun at high noon in august

a triangular sail swollen with milk
soars over a drifting corpse

it is august that soars
august apples tumble down the ridge

the lighthouse that died long ago
shines in the seamen's gaze

it is august that shines
the august fair comes close on first frost

the stone bell tolls on the seabed
its tolling stirs up the waves

the august sleepwalker
has seen the sun in the night

无 题

永远如此
火，是冬天的中心
当树林燃烧
只有那不肯围拢的石头
狂吠不已

挂在鹿角上的钟停了
生活是一次机会
仅仅一次
谁校对时间
谁就会突然衰老

UNTITLED

it has always been so
that fire is the center of winter
when the woods are ablaze
only stones that don't want to come closer
keep up their furious howl

the bell hanging on the deer's antlers has stopped ringing
life is one opportunity
a single one only
whoever checks the time
will find himself suddenly old

诗 艺

我所从属的那座巨大的房舍
只剩下桌子，周围
是无边的沼泽地
明月从不同的角度照亮我
骨骼松脆的梦依旧立在
远方，如尚未拆除的脚手架
还有白纸上泥泞的足印
那只喂养多年的狐狸
挥舞着火红的尾巴
赞美我，伤害我

当然，还有你，坐在我的对面
炫耀于你掌中的晴天的闪电
变成干柴，又化为灰烬

THE ART OF POETRY

in the great house to which I belong
only a table remains, surrounded
by boundless marshland
the moon shines on me from different corners
the skeleton's fragile dream still stands
in the distance, like an undismantled scaffold
and there are muddy footprints on the blank paper
the fox that has been fed for many years
with a flick of his fiery brush flatters and wounds me

and there is you, of course, sitting facing me
the fair-weather lightning that gleams in your palm
turns into firewood turns into ash

挽 歌

寡妇用细碎的泪水供奉着
偶像，等待哺乳的
是那群刚出生的饿狼
它们从生死线上一个个逃离
山峰耸动着，也传递了我的嚎叫
我们一起围困农场

你来自炊烟缭绕的农场
野菊花环迎风飘散
走向我，挺起小小而结实的乳房
我们相逢在麦地
小麦在花岗岩上疯狂地生长
你就是那寡妇，失去的

是我，是一生美好的愿望
我们躺在一起，汗水涔涔
床漂流在早晨的河上

DIRGE

before the idol, the widow makes an offering
of splintered tears; hungry wolfcubs
are waiting for mother's milk
one by one they have fled the line of life and death
heaving peaks pass on my howl
we besiege the farm together

leaving the farm wreathed in smoke
a ring of wild chrysanthemums nodding in the breeze
you walk toward me, small sturdy breasts outthrust
we meet in the fields
wheat growing wildly on granite cliffs
you are the widow, I

the lost, and lost a lifetime's precious longings
we lie together dripping sweat
the bed afloat on the morning river

空间

孩子们围坐在
环行山谷上
不知道下面是什么

纪念碑
在一座城市的广场
黑雨
街道空荡荡
下水道通向另一座
城市

我们围坐在
熄灭的火炉旁
不知道上面是什么

SPACE

the children sit in a circle
above a winding valley
not knowing what is below

a memorial column
in the town square
black rain
streets empty of man
sewers leading to another
town

we sit in a circle
around a dead stove
not knowing what is above

from OLD SNOW (1991)
translated by Bonnie S. McDougall and Chen Maiping

钟 声

钟声深入秋天的腹地
裙子纷纷落在树上
取悦着天空

我看见苹果腐烂的过程

带暴力倾向的孩子们
像黑烟一样升起
房瓦潮湿

十里风暴有了不倦的主人

沉默的敲钟人
展开的时间的幕布
碎裂，漫天飘零

一个个日子撞击不停

船只登陆
在大雪上滑行
一只绵羊注视着远方

它空洞的目光有如和平

万物正重新命名
尘世的耳朵
保持着危险的平衡

这是死亡的钟声

THE BELL

The bell tolls deep into autumn's hinterland
skirts scatter and fall on the trees
attempting to please the heavens

I watch the process of apples spoiling

children with a tendency to violence
ascend like black smoke
the roof tiles are damp

the three-mile storm has tireless masters

time's curtain
opened by the silent bellringer
disintegrates, adrift in the sky

the days strike, one endlessly after the other

boats land
sliding on the heavy snow
a sheep stares into the distance

its hollow gaze resembles peace

all things are being renamed
the ears of this mortal world
maintain a dangerous balance

It rings a death knell

晚 景

充了电的大海
船队满载着持灯的使者
逼近黑暗的细节

瞬间的刀锋
削掉一棵棵柏树上的火焰
枝干弯向更暗的一边

改变了夜的方向
山崖上的石屋
门窗开向四面八方

那些远道而来的灵魂
聚在光洁的瓷盘上
一只高脚蚊子站在中间

AN EVENING SCENE

On the electrified ocean
the fleet laden with messengers holding lamps
presses on toward the details of the dark

the moment's knife-edge
pares away the flames on each cypress
the branches curve toward the darker side

after having changed the night's direction
the stone house on the cliff
opens its doors and windows on all sides

the souls who've come from afar
collect on the bright clean china plate
a long-legged mosquito stands in the middle

无 题

比事故更陌生
比废墟更完整

说出你的名字
它永远弃你而去

钟表内部
留下青春的水泥

UNTITLED

more unfamiliar than an accident
more complete than ruins

having uttered your name
it abandons you forever

youth's mud is left behind
inside the clock

悼亡
　　——为六四受难者而作

不是生者是死者
在末日般殷殷红的天空下
结伴而行
苦难引导着苦难
恨的尽头是恨
泉水干涸，大火连绵
回去的路更远

不是上帝是孩子
在钢盔与钢盔撞击的
声音中祈祷
母亲孕育了光明
黑暗孕育了母亲
石头滚动，钟表倒转
日蚀已经出现

不是肉体是灵魂
每年一起再过一次生日
你们有同样的年龄
爱为死者缔造了
永久的联盟
你们紧紧拥抱
在长长的死亡名单中

REQUIEM
for the victims of June Fourth

Not the living but the dead
under the doomsday-purple sky
go in groups
suffering guides forward suffering
at the end of hatred is hatred
the spring has run dry, the conflagration stretches unbroken
the road back is even further away

Not gods but the children
amid the clashing of helmets
say their prayers
mothers breed light
darkness breeds mothers
the stone rolls, the clock runs backward
the eclipse of the sun has already taken place

Not your bodies but your souls
shall share a common birthday every year
you are all the same age
love has founded for the dead
an everlasting alliance
you embrace each other closely
in the massive register of deaths

在路上

七月，废弃的采石场
倾斜的风和五十只纸鹞掠过
向海跪下的人们
放弃了千年的战争

我调整时差
于是我穿过我的一生

欢呼自由
金沙的声音来自水中
腹中躁动的婴儿口含烟草
母亲的头被浓雾裹挟

我调整时差
于是我穿过我的一生

这座城市正在迁移
大大小小的旅馆排在铁轨上
游客们的草帽转动
有人向他们射击

我调整时差
于是我穿过我的一生

蜜蜂成群结队
追逐着流浪者飘移的花园
歌手与盲人
用双重光辉激荡夜空

我调整时差
于是我穿过我的一生

覆盖死亡的地图上
终点是一滴血
清醒的石头在我的脚下
被我遗忘

ALONG THE WAY

July, an abandoned stone quarry
the slanting wind and fifty paper hawks sweep by
the people kneeling toward the sea
have renounced their thousand year war

I adjust the time
so as to pass through my life

Hailing freedom
the sound of golden sands comes from water
the infant stirring in the belly has tobacco in its mouth
its mother's head is densely wrapped in fog

I adjust the time
so as to pass through my life

The city is migrating
hotels large and small are ranged on the tracks
the tourists' straw hats revolve
someone shoots at them

I adjust the time
so as to pass through my life

The bees in swarms
pursue the itinerants' drifting gardens
the singer and the blind man
agitate the night sky with their twofold glory

I adjust the time
so as to pass through my life

A drop of blood marks the final point
on the map spread over death
conscious stones underneath my feet
forgotten by me

过 节

毒蛇炫耀口中的钉子
大地有着毒蛇
吞吃鸟蛋的寂静
所有钟表
停止在无梦的时刻
丰收聚敛着
田野死后的笑容
从水银的镜子出发
影像成双的人们
乘家庭的轮子
去集市
一位本地英雄
在废弃的停车场上
唱歌

玻璃晴朗
桔子辉煌

CELEBRATING THE FESTIVAL*

The poisonous snake flaunts a nail in its mouth
on earth abides the silence
of snakes that swallow birds' eggs
all clocks and watches
stop at the dreamless moment
a bumper harvest gathers in
the smiling faces of dead fields
people with paired shadows
who set out from the mercury mirror
take the family wheels
to market
in an abandoned parking lot
a local hero
is singing

The glass shines bright
the orange gleams

* *Refers to June 4, 1989. The students occupying Tiananmen Square*
quoted Marx to the effect that revolution is the people's festival.

无 题

他睁开第三只眼睛
那颗头上的星辰
来自东西方相向的暖流
构成了拱门
高速公路穿过落日
两座山峰骑垮了骆驼
骨架被压进深深的
煤层

他坐在水下狭小的舱房里
压舱石般镇定
周围的鱼群光芒四射
自由那黄金的棺盖
高悬在监狱上方
在巨石后面排队的人们
等待着进入帝王的
记忆

词的流亡开始了

UNTITLED

He opens wide a third eye
the star above his head
warm currents from both east and west
have formed an archway
the expressway passes through the setting sun
two mountain peaks have ridden the camel to collapse
its skeleton has been pressed deep down
into a layer of coal

He sits in the narrow cabin underwater
calm as ballast
schools of fish around him flash and gleam
freedom, that golden coffin lid
hangs high above the prison
the people lining up behind the giant rock
are waiting to enter the emperor's
memory

The exile of words has begun

早晨的故事

一个词消灭了另一个词
一本书下令
烧掉了另一本书
语言的暴力建立的早晨
改变了早晨
人们的咳嗽声

蛆虫向果核进攻
果核来自迟钝的山谷
从迟钝的人群中
政府找到了它的发言人
猫与鼠
有相似的表情

空中之路
带枪的守林人查看
柏油的湖上
隆隆滚过的太阳
他听见灾难的声音
大火那纵情的声音

THE MORNING'S STORY

A word has abolished another word
a book has issued orders
to burn another book
a morning established by the violence of language
has changed the morning
of people's coughing

Maggots attack the kernel
the kernel comes from dull valleys
from among dull crowds
the government finds its spokesman
cats and mice
have similar expressions

On the road in the sky
the armed forester examines
the sun which rumbles past
over the asphalt lake
he hears the sound of disaster
the untrammelled sound of a great conflagration

旧雪

大雪复活了古老的语言
国家的版图变幻
在这块大陆上
一个异乡人的小屋
得到大雪的关怀

在我的门前
有一截三米长的钢轨

工厂倒闭，政府垮台
过期的报纸汇集着
变了质的大海
旧雪常来，新雪不来
造物的手艺失传
窗户后退
——五只喜鹊飞过

意外的阳光是一次事件

绿色的青蛙进入冬眠
这些邮差的罢工旷日持久
没有任何消息

OLD SNOW

When heavy snow revives an ancient language
maps of national territories change shape
on this continent
snow shows deep concern
for a foreigner's small room

Before my door
lies a three-meter-long steel rail

Factories go bankrupt, governments fall
outdated newspapers converge
into a decomposed ocean
old snow comes constantly, new snow comes not at all
the art of creation is lost
windows retreat
. . . five magpies fly past

Unexpected sunlight is an event

Green frogs start their hibernation
the postmen's strike drags on
no news of any kind

占 领

夜繁殖的一群蜗牛
闪闪发亮，逼近
人类的郊区
悬崖之间的标语写着：
未来属于你们

失眠已久的礁石
和水流暗合
导游的声音空旷：
这是敌人呆过的地方

少年跛脚而来
又跛脚奔向把守隘口的
方形的月亮

THE OCCUPATION

A troop of night-bred snails
glisten and shine, closing in
on humanity's outer suburbs
the poster hanging from cliff to cliff proclaims:
The future belongs to you

Insomnia-stricken reefs
conspire with streams
the tour guide's voice is vast:
This is where the enemy encamped

A youth limps forward
and sprints with a limp toward
the square moon guarding the pass

磨 刀

我借清晨的微光磨刀
发现刀背越来越薄
刀锋仍旧很钝
太阳一闪

大街上的人群
是巨大的橱窗里的树林
寂静轰鸣
我看见唱头正沿着
一棵树桩的年轮
滑向中心

WHETTING

When I whet a knife with dawn's faint light
I find the spine getting sharper
while the blade stays blunt
the sun flares

the crowds in the high street
are trees in huge shop windows
the silence roars
I see the stylus gliding
along the tree stump's rings
toward the center

此 刻

那伟大的进军
被一个精巧的齿轮
制止

从梦中领取火药的人
也领取伤口上的盐
和诸神的声音
余下的仅是永别
永别的雪
在夜空闪烁

AT THIS MOMENT

The great advance
is checked
by an ingenious gear

The man who gets gunpowder from dreams
also gets salt on his wounds
and gods' voices
the remainder is only farewell
farewell snow
gleams in the night sky

乡 音

我对着镜子说中文
一个公园有自己的冬天
我放上音乐
冬天没有苍蝇
我悠闲地煮着咖啡
苍蝇不懂什么是祖国
我加了点儿糖
祖国是一种乡音
我在电话线的另一端
听见了我的恐惧

A LOCAL ACCENT

I speak Chinese to the mirror
a park has its own winter
I put on music
winter is free of flies
I make coffee unhurriedly
flies don't understand what's meant by a native land
I add a little sugar
a native land is a kind of local accent
I hear my fright
on the other end of a phone line

巴赫音乐会

一颗罂粟籽挣脱了
鸟儿拨动风向的舌头
千匹红布从天垂落
人们迷失在
鲜艳的死亡中
巢穴空空
这是泄露天机的时刻

大教堂从波涛中升起
海下的山峰
带来史前的寂寞
左手变成玻璃
右手变成铁
我笨拙地鼓着掌
像一只登陆的企鹅

A BACH CONCERT

An opium-poppy seed struggles free from
the bird's tongue which bends the wind's direction
a thousand strips of red cloth hang from the sky
people lose their way in
brightly-colored death
the bird's nest is empty
it is time to reveal the secret

A great cathedral rises from the waves
the mountains under the sea
bring a prehistoric solitude
my left hand turns into glass
my right hand turns into iron
I clumsily clap my hands
like a penguin on dry land

画
　　　——给田田五岁生日

穿无袖连衣裙的早晨到来
大地四处滚动着苹果
我的女儿在画画
五岁的天空是多么辽阔
你的名字是两扇窗户
一扇开向没有指针的太阳
一扇开向你的父亲
他变成了逃亡的刺猬
带上几个费解的字
一只最红的苹果
离开了你的画
五岁的天空是多么辽阔

A PICTURE*

for Tiantian's fifth birthday

Morning arrives in a sleeveless dress
apples tumble all over the earth
my daughter is drawing a picture
how vast is a five-year-old sky
your name has two windows
one opens toward a sun with no clockhands
the other opens toward your father
who has become a hedgehog in exile
taking with him a few unintelligible characters
and a bright red apple
he has left your painting
how vast is a five-year-old sky

* *Tiantian, the nickname given to the poet's daughter, is written with two characters that look like a pair of windows. The same character also forms a part of the character for the word "picture."*

写作

始于河流而止于源泉

钻石雨
正在无情地剖开
这玻璃的世界

打开水闸，打开
刺在男人手臂上的
女人的嘴巴

打开那本书
词已磨损，废墟
有着帝国的完整

COMPOSITION

starts in the stream and stops at the source

diamond rain
is ruthlessly dissecting
the glass world

it opens the sluice, opens
a woman's lips
pricked on a man's arm

opens the book
the words have decomposed, the ruins
have imperial integrity

四 月

四月的风格不变：
鲜花加冰霜加抒情的翅膀

海浪上泡沫的眼睛
看见一把剪刀
藏在那风暴的口袋中

我双脚冰凉，在田野
那阳光鞣制的虎皮前止步

而头在夏天的闪电之间冥想
两只在冬天聋了的耳朵
向四周张望———

星星，那些小小的拳头
集结着浩大的游行

APRIL

April's style doesn't alter:
flowers plus frost plus lyrical wings

Bubbling eyes on the ocean
see a pair of scissors
hidden in the storm's pocket

My feet freeze, halting in front of
the field (a tiger skin tanned in the sun)

And my head ponders between flashes of summer lightning
my ears grown deaf during winter
gaze on all sides

Stars (these small fists)
combine to form a massive demonstration

叛逆者

那取悦于光的影子
引导我穿行在
饮过牛奶的白杨
和饮过血的狐狸之间
象条约穿行在
和平与阴谋之间

披外套的椅子坐在
东方，太阳是它的头
它打开一片云说：
这里是历史的终结
诸神退位，庙堂锁上
你仅仅是一个
失去声音的象形文字

REBEL

The shadow that tries to please the light
leads me to pass between
the aspen that has drunk milk
and the fox that has drunk blood
like a treaty passing between
peace and conspiracy

The chair draped with an overcoat sits
in the east, the sun is its head
it opens a cloud and says:
here is the end of history
the gods have abdicated, the temples are locked
you are nothing but
a pictograph that's lost its sound

from FORMS OF DISTANCE (1994)
translated by David Hinton

岁末

从一年的开始到终结
我走了多年
让岁月弯成了弓
到处是退休者的鞋
私人的尘土
公共的垃圾

这是并不重要的一年
铁锤闲着，而我
向以后的日子借光
瞥见一把白金尺
在铁砧上

YEAR'S END

from the year's beginning to its end
I've walked through countless years
time bending as a bow
shoes of those who've retired scattered
dust of the private
litter of the public

it's been a perfectly normal year
my sledgehammer sits idle, and yet
borrowing the light of the future
I glimpse that metric standard in platinum
here on the anvil

以 外

瓶中的风暴率领着大海前进
码头以外，漂浮的不眠之床上
拥抱的情人接上权力的链条
画框以外，带古典笑容的石膏像
以一日之内的阴影说话
信仰以外，骏马追上了死亡
月亮不停地在黑色事件上盖章
故事以外，一棵塑料树迎风招展
阴郁的粮食是我们生存的借口

BEYOND

a storm in a bottle is leading the sea's advance
beyond the harbor, on a floating bed of sleeplessness
embracing lovers link the chains of power
beyond the picture frame, a plaster figurine's classical smile
takes the shadow within day for speech
beyond conviction, a fast horse catches up with death
and the moon never stops leaving its seal on black events
beyond the story, a plastic tree flutters in the wind
that grain of gloom our pretext for existence

致托马斯·特朗斯特罗默

你把一首诗的最后一句
锁在心里———那是你的重心
随钟声摆动的教堂的重心
和无头的天使跳舞时
你保持住了平衡

你的大钢琴立在悬崖上
听众们紧紧抓住它
惊雷轰鸣，琴键疾飞
你回味着夜的列车
怎样追上了未来的黑暗

从蓝房子的车站出发
你冒雨去查看蘑菇
日与月，森林里的信号灯
七岁的彩虹后面
挤满戴着汽车面具的人

FOR T. TRANSTRÖMER

you take the poem's last line and
lock it center heart—it's your center of gravity
center of gravity in a church swinging among tolling bells
dancing with headless angels
you kept your balance

your grand piano's on clifftops
the audience grabbing it and holding tight
a crash of thunder strikes, a flight of keys
you wonder how that night train
caught up with tomorrow's darkness

leaving your blue train-station house
you brave rain to check mushrooms
sun and moon, forest signal lights
behind the seven-year-old rainbow
a capacity crowd's wearing automobiles as masks

走廊

那些啤酒瓶盖
被流动的大街输送到哪儿
那年我逃学，在电影院
在银幕无尽的走廊里
我突然被放大
那一刻是一把轮椅
其余的日子推着我远行——

全世界自由的代理人
把我输入巨型电脑：
一个潜入字典的外来语
一名持不同政见者
或一种与世界的距离

走廊尽头，某些字眼冒烟
被偷走玻璃的窗户
面对的是官僚的冬天

CORRIDOR

all those beer-bottle caps
where were they taken down moving streets
that year I cut class, in movie houses
inside the endless corridor of screens
I suddenly found myself enlarged
that moment was a wheelchair
and the days to come pushed me through distant travels—

the world's agents of freedom
entered me into their giant computer:
an alien voice sneaking into the dictionary
a dissident
perhaps a form of distance from the world

where the corridor ends, various words smolder
and a window robbed of its glass
faces the bureaucratic winter

苹果与顽石

大海的祈祷仪式
一个坏天气俯下了身

顽石空守五月
抵抗着绿色传染病

四季轮流砍伐着大树
群星在辨认道路

醉汉以他的平衡术
从时间中突围

一颗子弹穿过苹果
生活已被借用

APPLE AND BRUTE STONE

in the prayer ceremony of ocean
a storm bows down

stone watches over May in vain
guarding against that green contagion

as the four seasons take turns axing huge trees
stars try to recognize the road

a drunk using that talent for balance
breaks out from the time-siege

a bullet soars through the apple
life's on loan

战争状态

太阳密集地轰炸着大海
鲨鱼们在围攻下沉的岁月
那海底的银盘召唤家乡的传统：
带血的牛排，剥皮的土豆

进化史上不明的部分
是恋人们永远戒备的舌头
当密码严守人类的绝望
陌生的星球诞生了

荒草雇佣军占领了山谷
花朵缓慢地爆炸，树木生烟
我匍匐在诗歌后面
射击欢乐的鸟群

A STATE OF WAR

sunlight's hitting the sea with saturation bombing
sharks laying siege to the sinking years
that silver seafloor platter calls to hometown traditions:
steak rare, potatoes peeled

what remains unclear in evolutionary history
is the lover's ever vigilant tongue
in that secret code guarding human hopelessness
a strange planet was born

mercenary weeds captured mountain valleys
blossoms casually detonate, trees smoke
I lie behind song
firing into cheery flocks of birds

无 题

苍鹰的影子掠过
麦田战栗

我成为夏天的解释者
回到大路上
戴上帽子集中思想

如果天空不死

UNTITLED

hawk shadow flickers past
fields of wheat shiver

I'm becoming one who explicates summer
return to the main road
put on a cap to concentrate thoughts

if deep skies never die

忧 郁

我乘电梯从地下停车场
升到海平线的位置
冥想继续上升，越过蓝色

像医生一样不可阻挡
他们，在决定我的一生：
通向成功的道路

男孩子的叫喊与季节无关
他在成长，他知道
怎样在梦里伤害别人

FORLORN

I take the elevator from an underground parking lot
up to sea level
deep thoughts continuing up, through blue color

like doctors you can't stop
them, deciding my whole life:
the road to success

the season's unrelated to a boy's shout
he's growing up, he knows
how to wound others in his dreams

夜 巡

他们的天空，我的睡眠
黑暗中的演讲者

在冬天转车
在冬天转车
养蜂人远离他的花朵

另一个季节在停电
小小的祭品啊
不同声部的烛火

老去已不可能，老去的
半路，老虎回头——

NIGHT PATROL

their skies, my sleep
and orators in the midst of darkness

changing trains in winter
changing trains in winter
the beekeeper far from his flowers

in the power outage another season
o tiny offerings
candle flames in different parts of the chorus

grown old impossible, on that grown-old
road, an old tiger turns back—

毒 药

烟草屏住呼吸

流亡者的窗户对准
大海深处放飞的翅膀
冬日的音乐驶来
像褪色的旗帜

是昨天的风，是爱情

悔恨如大雪般降落
当一块石头裸露出结局
我以此刻痛哭余生

再给我一个名字

我伪装成不幸
遮挡母语的太阳

TOXIN

tobacco's breath catches short

an exile's window aims at
deep-sea wings released into flight
music of a winter's day sailing closer
like a flag shedding its colors

it's yesterday's wind, it's love

remorse deep as the fall of heavy snow
when a stone reveals the end result
I take this moment to weep for the rest of my life

give me another name

I've made a disguise of misfortune
shelter from the mother tongue's solar blaze

在天涯

群山之间的爱情

永恒，正如万物的耐心
简化人的声音
一声凄厉的叫喊
从远古至今

休息吧，疲惫的旅行者
受伤的耳朵
暴露了你的尊严

一声凄厉的叫喊

AT THE SKY'S EDGE

love among the mountains

eternity, that patience of the earth
simplifies our human sounds
one arctic-thin cry
from deep antiquity until now

rest, weary traveler
a wounded ear's
already laid your dignity bare

one arctic-thin cry

醒 悟

成群的乌鸦再次出现
冲向行军的树林

我在冬天的斜坡上醒来
梦在向下滑行

有时阳光仍保持
两只狗见面时的激动

那交响乐是一所医院
整理着尘世的混乱

老人突然撒手
一生织好的布匹

水涌上枝头
金属的玫瑰永不凋零

AWAKENING

flocks of crows appear once again
invading the marching forest

I come to on the slope of winter
dream gliding downhill

there are times sunlight still holds
the exhilaration of two dogs meeting

that symphony a hospital
sorting through this world of confusion

an old man suddenly lets go of that
cloth he spent a lifetime weaving

water wells up to the tips of branches
a metal rose never withers

新世纪

倾心于荣耀，大地转暗
我们读混凝土之书的
灯光，读真理

金子的炸弹爆炸
我们情愿成为受害者
把伤口展示给别人

考古学家会发现
底片上的时代幽灵
一个孩子抓住它，说不

是历史妨碍我们飞行
是鸟妨碍我们走路
是腿妨碍我们做梦

是我们诞生了我们
是诞生

A NEW CENTURY

in love with glory, the earth grows dark
reading the lights of a concrete
book, we read truth

solid gold bombs detonate
and we're glad to be victims
showing our wounds to the others

when archaeologists discover
the ghost of the era on a negative
a child grabs it, saying no

it's history that won't let us fly
it's birds that won't let us walk
it's legs that won't let us dream

it's our giving birth to ourselves
it's birth

问天

今夜雨零乱
清风翻书
字典旁敲侧击
逼我就范

从小背古诗
不得要领
阐释的深渊旁
我被罚站

月朗星稀
老师的手从中
指点迷津
影子戏仿人生

有人在教育
的斜坡上滑雪
他们的故事
滑出国界

词滑出了书
白纸是遗忘症
我洗净双手
撕碎它，雨停

ASKING THE SKY

tonight a confusion of rain
fresh breezes leaf through the book
dictionaries swell with implication
forcing me into submission

memorizing ancient poems as a child
I couldn't see what they meant
and stood at the abyss of explication
for punishment

bright moon sparse stars
out of those depths a teacher's hands
give directions to the lost
a shadow mocking our lives

people slide down the slope of
education on skis
their story
slides beyond national boundaries

after words slide beyond the book
the white page is pure amnesia
I wash my hands clean
and tear it apart, the rain stops

忠 诚

别开灯
黑暗之门引来圣者

我的手熟知途径
像一把旧钥匙
在心的位置
打开你的命运

三月在门外飘动

几根竹子摇晃
有人正从地下潜泳
暴风雪已过
蝴蝶重新集结

我信仰般追随你
你追随死亡

ALLEGIANCE

don't turn the lights on
darkness is a door bringing the saint near

my hand knows the way perfectly
like an old key
at the heart-site
opening your destiny

March flutters outside the door

a few bamboo sway
people snorkeling underground
now the snowstorm's passed
butterflies gather again

it's my faith to be following you
you following death

无 题

在母语的防线上
奇异的乡愁
垂死的玫瑰

玫瑰用茎管饮水
如果不是水
至少是黎明

最终露出午夜
疯狂的歌声
披头散发

UNTITLED

at the mother tongue's line of defense
a strange homesickness
a dying rose

rose sipping water via stem-tubing
or if it isn't water
it's at least dawn light

revealing midnight in the end
wild song
flurried head of hair

一幅肖像

为信念所伤，他来自八月
那危险的母爱
被一面镜子夺去
他侧身于犀牛与政治之间
像裂缝隔开时代

哦同谋者，我此刻
只是一个普通的游客
在博物馆大厅的棋盘上
和别人交叉走动

激情不会过时
但访问必须秘密进行
我突然感到那琴弦的疼痛
你调音，为我奏一曲
在众兽涌入历史之前

A PORTRAIT

wounded by convictions, he came from August
a mother's perilous love
stolen away by a mirror
he's sideways between the rhinoceros and politics
like a fissure separating epochs

o conspirators, I'm nothing now
but a common wanderer
walking the cavernous museum's chessboard
trading places with strangers

great passion's never outdated
but our visits require secrecy
suddenly I feel the ache of strings
you're tuning, play me a song
before predators emerge into history

关于永恒

从众星租来的光芒下
长跑者穿过死城

和羊谈心
我们共同分享美酒
和桌下的罪行

雾被引入夜歌
炉火如伟大的谣言
迎向风

如果死是爱的理由
我们爱不贞之情
爱失败的人
那察看时间的眼睛

ON ETERNITY

beneath a radiance rented from the stars
long-distance runners transit death's city

chatting heart-to-heart with sheep
we share a lovely wine
and under-the-table crime

fog's lured into night-song
and stove-fire like mighty rumor
greets the wind

if death's the reason for love
we love unfaithful passion
love the defeated
those eyes gazing into time

from LANDSCAPE OVER ZERO (1996)
translated by David Hinton and Yanbing Chen

另一个

这棋艺平凡的天空
看海水变色
楼梯深入镜子
盲人学校里的手指
触摸鸟的消亡

这闲置冬天的桌子
看灯火明灭
记忆几度回首
自由射手们在他乡
听历史的风声

某些人早已经匿名
或被我们阻拦在
地平线以下
而另一个在我们之间
突然嚎啕大哭

ANOTHER

this sky unexceptional at chess
watches the sea change color
a ladder goes deep into the mirror
fingers in a school for the blind
touch the extinction of birds

look at those flickering lights
on winter's fallow table
memory looks back a few times
the archer of freedom in foreign lands
listen to history's wind

some abandoned their names long ago
or we stalled them
under the horizon
meanwhile another among us
bursts into tears

蓝 墙

道路追问天空

一只轮子
寻找另一只轮子作证:

这温暖的皮毛
闪电之诗
生殖和激情
此刻或缩小的全景
无梦

是汽油的欢乐

BLUE WALL

road chases sky asking

one wheel
seeks another to bear witness

this pelt of warmth
poetry of lightning
procreation and passion
this very moment or whole vistas reduced
dreamless

are gasoline's thrills

背景

必须修改背景
你才能够重返故乡

时间撼动了某些字
起飞，又落下
没透露任何消息
一连串的失败是捷径
穿过大雪中寂静的看台
逼向老年的大钟

而一个家庭宴会的高潮
和酒精的含量有关
离你最近的女人
总是带着历史的愁容
注视着积雪，　空行

田鼠们所坚信的黑暗

BACKGROUND

the background needs revising
you can return to your hometown

a few time-shaken words
lift into flight, fall back
divulging no news whatsoever
a string of failures is the shortcut
past silent grandstands in heavy snow
pressing toward the huge clock of old age

at the family gathering
high tide is a matter of alcohol content
the woman closest to you
always wears the worried look of history
gazes into snowdrifts, double space to

darkness in which voles believe absolutely

无 题

在父亲平坦的想象中
孩子们固执的叫喊
终于撞上了高山
不要惊慌
我沿着某些树的想法
从口吃转向歌唱

来自远方的悲伤
是一种权力
我用它锯桌子
有人为了爱情出发
而一座宫殿追随风暴
驶过很多王朝

带家具的生活
此外，跳蚤擂动大鼓
道士们练习升天
青春深入小巷
为夜的逻辑而哭
我得到休息

UNTITLED

in the plains of a father's imagination
insistent cries of children
strike high peaks in the end
don't panic
tracing thoughts of certain trees
I stutter into song

sorrow from far away
is a kind of power
I use it to saw tables
someone sets out for the sake of love
and a palace following storms
sails through many dynasties

beyond life with home
furnishings, fleas beat a huge drum
Taoists practice their ascent into heaven
youth goes deep into back alleys
weeping over the logic of night
I attain rest

这一天

风熟知爱情
夏日闪烁着皇家的颜色
钓鱼人孤独地测量
大地的伤口
敲响的钟在膨胀
午后的漫步者
请加入这岁月的含义

有人俯向钢琴
有人扛着梯子走过
睡意被推迟了几分钟
仅仅几分钟
太阳在研究阴影
我从明镜饮水
看见心目中的敌人

男高音的歌声
像油轮激怒大海
我凌晨三时打开罐头
让那些鱼大放光明

THIS DAY

wind knows what love is
the summer day flashing royal colors
a lone fisherman surveys
the world's wound
a struck bell swells
people strolling in the afternoon
please join the year's implications

someone bends toward a piano
someone carries a ladder past
sleepiness has been postponed a few minutes
only a few minutes
the sun researches shadow
and drinking water from a bright mirror
I see the enemy within

an oil tanker
the tenor's song enrages the sea
at three in the morning I open a tin can
setting some fish on fire

二月

夜正趋于完美
我在语言中漂流
死亡的乐器
充满了冰

谁在日子的裂缝上
歌唱，水变苦
火焰失血
山猫般奔向星星
必有一种形式
才能做梦

在早晨的寒冷中
一只觉醒的鸟
更接近真理
而我和我的诗
一起下沉

书中的二月：
某些动作与阴影

FEBRUARY

night approaching perfection
I float amid languages
the brasses in death's music
full of ice

who's up over the crack in day
singing, water turns bitter
bled flames pale
leaping like leopards toward stars
to dream
you need a form

in the cold morning
an awakened bird
comes closer to truth
as I and my poems
sink together

february in the book:
certain movements and shadows

我们

失魂落魄
提着灯笼追赶春天

伤疤发亮，杯子转动
光线被创造
看那迷人的时刻：
盗贼潜入邮局
信发出叫喊

钉子啊钉子
这歌词不可更改
木柴紧紧搂在一起
寻找听众

寻找冬天的心
河流尽头
船夫等待着茫茫暮色

必有人重写爱情

WE

lost souls and scattered spirits
holding lanterns chase spring

scars shimmer, cups revolve
light's being created
look at that enchanting moment
a thief steals into a post office
letters cry out

nails o nails
the lyrics never change
firewood huddles together
searching for an audience to listen

searching for the heart of winter
river's end
a boatman awaiting boundless twilight

there must be someone to rewrite love

明 镜

夜半饮酒时
真理的火焰发疯
回首处
谁没有家
窗户为何高悬

你倦于死
道路倦于生
在那火红的年代
有人昼伏夜行
与民族对弈

并不止于此
挖掘你睡眠的人
变成蓝色
早晨倦于你
明镜倦于词语

想想爱情
你有如壮士
惊天动地之处
你对自己说
太冷

BRIGHT MIRROR

in the midnight hour of wine
the flame of truth gets crazy
a place for looking back
who has no home
why do windows loom so high

you're tired of death
the road's tired of life
in those flame-red times
someone rests by day and travels by night
playing chess with a nation

but that's not all
people excavating your sleep
turn blue
morning's tired of you
the bright mirror's tired of words

think about love
and you're like some hero
where heaven trembles and earth shakes
you say to yourself
too cold

早 晨

那些鱼内脏如灯
又亮了一次

醒来，口中含盐
好似初尝喜悦

我出去散步
房子学会倾听

一些树转身
某人成了英雄

必须用手势问候
鸟和打鸟的人

MORNING

those fish entrails as if lights
blink again

waking, there's salt in my mouth
just like the first taste of joy

I go out for a walk
houses learning to listen

a few trees turn around
and someone's become a hero

you must use hand gestures to greet
birds and the hunters of birds

据我所知

前往那故事中的人们
搬开了一座大山
他才诞生

我从事故出发
刚抵达另一个国家
颠倒字母
使每餐必有意义

踮脚够着时间的刻度
战争对他还太远
父亲又太近
他低头通过考试
踏上那无边的甲板

隔墙有耳
但我要跟上他的速度
写作!

他用红色油漆道路
让凤凰们降落
展示垂死的动作
那些含义不明的路标
环绕着冬天
连音乐都在下雪

我小心翼翼
每个字下都是深渊

当一棵大树
平息着八面来风
他的花园
因妄想而荒芜

我漫不经心地翻看
他的不良记录
只能坚信过去的花朵

AS FAR AS I KNOW

people on the way to that story
moved a mountain
then he was born

setting out from the accident
I barely reached another country
turning alphabets upside down
to fill every meal with meaning

he reaches up to the scale measuring time
war remains too far away
father too close
he stoops to pass through exams
and boards that boundless boatdeck

someone's listening behind walls
I must hurry to keep up with him
writing!

he paints the road red
lets phoenixes land
flaunting death throes
those incoherent roadsigns
surround winter
snow falling even from music

I'm careful very careful
there's an abyss beneath every word

when a huge tree
quiets wind from the eights directions
his flower garden
is desolated by fantasy

I leaf carelessly through
his bad record
nothing to believe but the past's flower

他伪造了我的签名
而长大成人
并和我互换大衣
以潜入我的夜
搜寻着引爆故事的
导火索

he forged my signature
and grew into a man
traded coats with me
and stole into my night
searching out the story's detonation
fuse

守夜

月光小于睡眠
河水穿过我们的房间
家具在哪儿靠岸

不仅是编年史
也包括非法的气候中
公认的一面
使我们接近雨林
哦哭泣的防线

玻璃镇纸读出
文字叙述中的伤口
多少黑山挡住了
一九四九年

在无名小调的尽头
花握紧拳头叫喊

NIGHTWATCH

moonlight smaller than sleep
the river flows through our room
where is furniture docking

not only annals of history
but also the illicit climate's
acknowledged aspects
bring us to rain forests
o line of defense in tears

glass paperweights decode
writing's wound of narration
how many black mountains blocked
1949

where a nameless tune ends
blossoms scream clenched fists

无 题

人们赶路，到达
转世，隐入鸟之梦
太阳从麦田逃走
又随乞丐返回

谁与天比高
那早夭的歌手
在气象图里飞翔
掌灯冲进风雪

我买了份报纸
从日子找回零钱
在夜的入口处
摇身一变

被颂扬之鱼
穿过众人的泪水
喂，上游的健康人
到明天有多远

UNTITLED

people hurry on, arrive
return in another life, fade into bird dreams
the sun flees wheat fields
then comes back trailing after beggars

who's rivaled sky for height
that singer who died young
soars in the weather map
flies into snowstorms holding a lamp

I bought a newspaper
got change back from the day
and at the entrance to night
eased into a new identity

celebrated fish
move through everyone's tears
hey, you folks upstream achievers so hale and hearty
how far is it to tomorrow

无 题

几度诗中回首
夜鸟齐鸣
你向歌声逝去之外
释放着烟雾

打伞进入明天
你, 漫游者
从你的尽头再向前
什么能替代喜悦

世機纪的狐狸们
在鸿沟之间跳跃
你看见那座辉煌的鏒桥
怎样消失在天边

一个早晨触及
核桃隐秘的思想
水的激情之上
是云初醒时的孤独

UNTITLED

looking back a few times in the poem
night birds singing together
you set smoke drifting free
toward a place where song vanishes

walking into tomorrow beneath an umbrella
you, a wanderer
set out from your own end
what can replace joy

the century's foxes
leap from abyss to abyss
you see how that glorious bridge
disappears at the sky's edge

morning touches
the secret thought of a walnut
above the passion of water
it's the loneliness of cloud waking

旧地

死亡总是从反面
观察一幅画

此刻我从窗口
看见我年轻时的落日
旧地重游
我急于说出真相
可在天黑前
又能说出什么

饮过词语之杯
更让人干渴
与河水一起援引大地
我在空山倾听
吹笛人内心的呜咽

税收的天使们
从画的反面归来
从那些镀金的头颅
一直清点到落日

OLD PLACES

death's always on the other side
watching the painting

at the window just now
I saw a sunset from my youth
visiting old places again
I'm anxious to tell the truth
but before the skies go dark
what more can be said

drinking a cup of words
only makes you thirstier
I join riverwater to quote the earth
and listen in empty mountains
to the flute player's sobbing heart

angels collecting taxes
return from the painting's other side
from those gilded skulls
taking inventory clear into sunset

下一棵树

风从哪儿来
我们数着罂粟籽中的
日日夜夜

大雪散布着
某一气流的谎言
邮筒醒来
信已改变含义
道路通向历史以外
我们牵回往事
拴在下一棵树上

来吧，野蛮人
请加入这一传说
这预订的时刻开花
谦卑的火焰
变成他乡之虎

我们游遍四方
总是从下一棵树出发
返回，为了命名
那路上的忧伤

THE NEXT TREE

where is it wind comes from
we count days and nights passing
inside poppy seeds

a huge snowstorm spreads
that lie a certain flow of air tells
a mailbox wakes
letters already meaning something else
the road leads somewhere beyond history
we shepherd old memories out
and hitch them to the next tree

come, you barbarians
please join this legend
this moment reserved in advance blooms
humble flames
becoming a tiger in a foreign land

we've traveled everywhere
always setting out from the next tree
and returning, just to name
that sorrow of the road

为了

不眠之灯引导着你
从隐藏的棋艺中
找到对手

歌声兜售它的影子
你从某个结论
走向开放的黎明
为什么那最初的光线
让你如此不安？

一棵被种进伤口的
种子拒绝作证：
你因期待而告别
因爱而受苦

激情，正如轮子
因闲置而完美

FOR THE PURPOSE OF

a sleepless lamp leads you
to search out an opponent
in the hidden art of chess

song peddles its shadow
from a certain conclusion
you walk toward the opening dawn
why is it the earliest gleam
makes you so anxious?

a seed planted inside wounds
refuses to bear witness:
you leave whenever you expect more
suffer whenever you love

passion, just like a wheel
grows perfect whenever it's idle

无 题

当语言发疯，我们
在法律的一块空地上
因聋哑而得救
一辆辆校车
从光的深渊旁驶过
夜是一部旧影片
琴声如雨浸润了时代

孤儿们追逐着蓝天
服丧的书肃立
在通往阐释之路上
杜鹃花及姐妹们
为死亡而开放

UNTITLED

when language was insane, we
stood in the law's one vacant lot
and being deaf and dumb were saved
one school bus after another
skirts past an abyss of light
night's an old movie
and music soaks into the age like rain

as orphans chase blue sky
books stand in mourning
on the road leading to explanation
azalea and her sisters
bloom for death

零度以上的风景

是鹞鹰教会歌声游泳
是歌声追溯那最初的风

我们交换欢乐的碎片
从不同的方向进入家庭

是父亲确认了黑暗
是黑暗通向经典的闪电

哭泣之门砰然关闭
回声在追赶它的叫喊

是笔在绝望中开花
是花反抗着必然的旅程

是爱的光线醒来
照亮零度以上的风景

LANDSCAPE OVER ZERO

it's hawk teaching song to swim
it's song tracing back to the first wind

we trade scraps of joy
enter family from different directions

it's a father confirming darkness
it's darkness leading to that lightning of the classics

a door of weeping slams shut
echoes chasing its cry

it's a pen blossoming in lost hope
it's a blossom resisting the inevitable route

it's love's gleam waking to
light up landscape over zero

不对称

历史的诡计之花开放
忙于演说的手指受伤
攒下来的阳光成为年龄
你沉于往事和泡沫
埋葬愤怒的工具
一个来自过去的陌生人
从镜子里指责你

而我所看到的是
守城的昏鸦正一只只死去
教我呼吸和意义的老师
在我写作的阴影咳血
那奔赴节日的衣裙
随日蚀或完美的婚姻
升起，没有歌声

ASYMMETRY

the blossom of history's ruse opens
fingers busy with talk are wounded
hoarded sunlight becomes age
you drown in times past and bubbles
bury anger's tools
a stranger out of the past
chides you from the mirror

though what I've seen is
the city's dusky guardian-crows dying one by one
and those who taught me breath and meaning
coughing up blood in shadows my writing casts
dresses rushing toward holidays
follow solar eclipse and perfect marriage
& rise, songless

关键词

我的影子很危险
这受雇于太阳的艺人
带来的最后的知识
是空的

那是蛀虫工作的
黑暗属性
暴力的最小的孩子
空中的足音

关键词，我的影子
锤打着梦中之铁
踏着那节奏
一只孤狼走进

无人失败的黄昏
鹭鸶在水上书写
一生一天一个句子
结束

KEYWORD

my shadow's dangerous
this craftsman the sun hired
brings final knowledge
it's empty

that's the dark nature of
a moth's hungry work
smallest child of violence
footsteps in air

keyword my shadow
hammers dreamworld iron
stepping to that rhythm
a lone wolf walks into

dusk of no one's defeat
an egret writes on water
a life a day a sentence
ends

远 景

海鸥，尖叫的梦
抗拒着信仰的天空
当草变成牛奶
风失去细节

若风是乡愁
道路就是其言说

在道路尽头
一只历史的走狗
扮装成夜
正向我逼近

夜的背后
有无边的粮食
伤心的爱人

THE LONG VIEW

seagulls, shriek dream
resisting skies of belief
when pasture becomes milk
wind loses detail

if wind is the longing for home
roads must be its speech

at the far end of the road
history's stooge
masquerades as night
and closes in on me

out back of night
it's boundless grain
heartbreak lover

边 境

风暴转向北方的未来
病人们的根在地下怒吼
太阳的螺旋桨
驱赶蜜蜂变成光芒
链条上的使者们
在那些招风耳里播种

被记住的河流
不再终结
被偷去了的声音
已成为边境

边境上没有希望
一本书
吞下一个翅膀
还有语言的坚冰中
赎罪的兄弟
你为此而斗争

BORDERS

storms turn toward the north's future
sick people's roots howl underground
a sun propeller
chases bees until they're rays of light
messengers in chains
sow seed in those ears long for the wind

remembered rivers
never end
stolen sound
becomes borders

borders allow no hope
a book
swallows a wing
and still in the hard ice of language
brothers redeem their crimes
you struggle on for this

新 年

怀抱花朵的孩子走向新年
为黑暗文身的指挥啊
在倾听那最短促的停顿

快把狮子关进音乐的牢笼
快让石头伪装成隐士
在平行之间移动

谁是客人？当所有的日子
倾巢而出在路上飞行
失败之书博大精深

每一刻都是捷径
我得以穿过东方的意义
回家，关上死亡之门

NEW YEAR

a child carrying flowers walks toward the new year
a conductor tattooing darkness
listens to the shortest pause

hurry a lion into the cage of music
hurry stone to masquerade as a recluse
moving in parallel nights

who's the visitor? when the days all
tip from nests and fly down roads
the book of failure grows boundless and deep

each moment a shortcut
I follow it through the meaning of the East
returning home, closing death's door

无 题

醒来是自由
那星辰之间的矛盾

门在抵抗岁月
丝绸卷走了叫喊
我是被你否认的身份
从心里关掉的灯

这脆弱的时刻
敌对的岸
风折叠所有的消息
记忆变成了主人

哦陈酒
因表达而变色
煤会遇见必然的矿灯
火不能为火作证

UNTITLED

in waking there is freedom
that contradiction among stars

doors resisting the years
silk carried screams away
I'm the identity you deny
lamp switched off in the heart

this fragile moment
hostile shores
wind folds up all the news
memory's become master

o vintage wine
changing color for clear expression
coal meets the miner's inevitable lamp
fire cannot bear witness to fire

冬之旅

谁在虚无上打字
太多的故事
是十二块石头
击中表盘
是十二只天鹅
飞离冬天

而夜里的石头
描述着光线
盲目的钟
为缺席者呼喊

进入房间
你看见那个丑角
在进入冬天时
留下的火焰

WINTER TRAVELS

who's typing on the void
too many stories
they're twelve stones
hitting the clockface
twelve swans
flying out of winter

tongues in the night
describe gleams of light
blind bells
cry out for someone absent

entering the room
you see that jester's
entered winter
leaving behind flame

休息

你终于到达
云朵停靠的星期天

休息，正如慌言
必须小心有人窥看

它在键盘上弹奏
白昼与黑夜

弹奏明天
那幸福的链条

死者挣脱了影子
锁住天空

REST

you finally arrive
at the sunday where clouds moor

rest, just like a lie
make sure no one's watching

it's performing on a keyboard
days white and nights black

performing tomorrow
that chain of happiness

the dead broke free of shadow
and locked up the sky

工作

　　与它的影子竞赛
　　鸟变成了回声

　　并非偶然，你
　　在风暴中选择职业
　　是飞艇里的词
　　古老的记忆中的
　　刺

　　开窗的母亲
　　像旧书里的主人公
　　展开秋天的折扇
　　如此耀眼

　　你这不肖之子
　　用白云擦洗玻璃
　　擦洗玻璃中的自己

WORK

competing with its shadow
a bird becomes echo

not unexpectedly, you
choosing a profession in the storm
are the word inside zeppelins
ancient memory's
thorn

mother opening windows
like some hero in an old book
spreads autumn's fan open
dazzling the eyes

you unfilial son
wiping glass clean with white cloud
wiping the self in glass clean

旅行

那影子在饮水
那笑声模仿
撑开黎明的光线的
崩溃方式

带着书去旅行
书因旅行获得年龄
因旅行而匿名
那深入布景的马
回首

你刚好到达
那人出生的地方

鱼从水下看城市
水下有新鲜的诱饵
令人难堪的锚

JOURNEY

that shadow's drinking water
laughter mimics
the dawn-opening gleam's
collapsing ways

you set out on a journey with books
books age because of journeys
hide their names because of journeys
that horse deep in the stage scenery
turns its head

you've just arrived
at that person's birthplace

fish watch the city from underwater
among fresh bait underwater
there's an embarrassing anchor

from UNLOCK (2000)
translated by Eliot Weinberger and Iona Man-Cheong

六月

风在耳边说，六月
六月是张黑名单
我提前离席

请注意告别方式
那些词的叹息

请注意那些诠释：
无边的塑料花
在死亡左岸
水泥广场
从写作中延伸

到此刻
我从写作中逃跑
当黎明被锻造
旗帜盖住大海

而忠实于大海的
低音喇叭说，六月

JUNE

Wind at the ear says *June*
June a blacklist I slipped
in time

note this way to say goodbye
the sighs within these words

note these annotations:
unending plastic flowers
on the dead left bank
the cement square extending
from writing to

now
I run from writing
as dawn is hammered out
a flag covers the sea

and loudspeakers loyal to the sea's
deep bass say *June*

阅 读

品尝多余的泪水
你的星宿啊
照耀着迷人的一天

一双手是诞生中
最抒情的部分
一个变化着的字
在舞蹈中
寻找它的根

看夏天的文本
那饮茶人的月亮
正是废墟上
乌鸦弟子们的
黄金时间

所有跪下的含义
损坏了指甲
所有生长的烟
加入了人的诺言

品尝多余的大海
背叛的盐

READING

Taste the unnecessary tears
your star stays
alit still for one charmed day

a hand is birth's
most expressive thing
a word changes
dancing
in search of its roots

read the text of summer
the moonlight from which
that person drinks tea
is the true golden age
for disciples of crows in the ruins

all the subservient meanings
broke fingernails
all the growing smoke
seeped into the promises

taste the unnecessary sea
the salt betrayed

安魂曲
　　——给珊珊

那一年的浪头
淹没了镜中之沙
迷途即离别
而在离别的意义上
所有语言的瞬间
如日影西斜

生命只是个诺言
别为它悲伤
花园毁灭以前
我们有过太多时间
争辩飞鸟的含义
敲开午夜之门

孤独像火柴被擦亮
当童年的坑道
导向可疑的矿层
迷途即离别
而诗在纠正生活
纠正诗的回声

REQUIEM
for Shanshan

The wave of that year
flooded the sands on the mirror
to be lost is a kind of leaving
and the meaning of leaving
the instant when all languages
are like shadows cast from the west

life's only a promise
don't grieve for it
before the garden was destroyed
we had too much time
debating the implications of a bird flying
as we knocked down midnight's door

alone like a match polished into light
when childhood's tunnel
led to a vein of dubious ore
to be lost is a kind of leaving
and poetry rectifying life
rectifies poetry's echo

送报

谁相信面具的哭泣
谁相信哭泣的国家
国家失去记忆
记忆成为早晨

送报的孩子从早晨出发
凄厉的小号响遍全城
是你的不幸还是我的不幸
神经脆弱的蔬菜啊
农民们把手栽进地里
盼望抓住金条的好年景
政客在自己舌头上
撒着胡椒粉
而桦树林正在讨论
是捐献于艺术还是门

这个公共的早晨
被送报的小孩所创造
一场革命掠过街头
他睡着了

DELIVERING NEWSPAPERS

Who believes in the mask's weeping?
who believes in the weeping nation?
the nation has lost its memory
memory goes as far as this morning

the newspaper boy sets out in the morning
all over town the sound of a desolate trumpet
is it your bad omen or mine?
vegetables with fragile nerves
peasants plant their hands in the ground
longing for the gold of a good harvest
politicians sprinkle pepper
on their own tongues
and a stand of birches in the midst of a debate:
whether to sacrifice themselves for art or doors

this public morning
created by a paperboy
revolution sweeps past the corner
he's fast asleep

古 堡

那些玫瑰令人羞惭
像这家族的真理
让你久久逗留

喷泉追溯到生殖
黑暗的第一线光明
死水吞吃浮雕上
骄傲的火焰

松裹的迷宫是语法
你找到出路才会说话
沿着一级级台阶
深入这语言的内部
明门暗道通向
那回声般的大厅

你高喊，没有回声

在环绕你的肖像中
最后一代女主人
移开她老年的面具

在情欲之杯饮水
她目送一只猫
走出那生命的界限
零度，琴声荡漾
他人的时刻表
不再到达的明天

1916年。战争箭头
指往所有方向
她铺上雪白的桌布
召唤饥饿的艺术
当最后的烛火
陈述着世纪的风暴
她死于饥饿

THE OLD CASTLE

Those roses a cause of shame
like the truth of this clan
letting you linger for a long while

the fountain traces back the first thread of light
in the darkness of reproduction
stagnant water swallows
the arrogant flame on the carved relief

the pine hedge labyrinth is a grammar
find the way out and you can speak
follow the flight of stairs
deep into this language
unobstructed corridors and hidden passages
lead to that echoing hall

you shout out loud, there is no echo

portraits surround you
the last generation of hostesses
slip off their old-age masks

drinking water from desire's cup
her eyes carry a cat
beyond the boundaries of life

zero degrees, sound of a piano rippling
someone else's calendar
a tomorrow that never returns

1916: the arrowheads of war
point in all directions
she spreads the white tablecloth
to invoke the art of starvation
as the light of the last candle
reports the century's storm
she dies of starvation

井，大地的独眼

你触摸烛台
那双冰冷的手
握住火焰
她喂养过的鸽子
在家族的沉默作窝

听到明天的叹息
大门砰然关闭
艺术已死去
玫瑰刚刚开放

a well, the earth's single eye

you touch the candlestick
that frozen hand
gripping the flame
the pigeons she raised
make their nest in the clan silence

hearing the sighs of tomorrow
the main gate clangs shut
art is dead
roses bloom

无 题

小号如尖锐的犁
耕种夜：多久
阳光才会破土

多久那聆听者才会
转身，看到我们
多久我们才会
通过努力
成为我们的荣耀

直到谷粒入仓
这思想不属于谁
那有此刻与来世的
落差：巨浪拍岸
我们与青春为邻
听狂暴心跳

在更空旷的地方
睡眠塞满稻草

UNTITLED

A trumpet like a sharp plow
tills the night: how long
till sunlight breaks the ground?

how long till those who listen respectfully
turn around and see us?
how long till we
through effort and exertion
turn into glory?

till the grain goes into the granary
this thought belongs to no one
a drop in the water-level between
this moment and the next life:
huge waves beat against the shore
next door to youth
we hear the wild palpitations

in a space even vaster
sleep stuffed with rice straw

岗 位

一只麋鹿走向陷阱
权力，枞树说，斗争

怀着同一秘密
我头发白了
退休——倒退着
离开我的岗位

只退了一步
不，整整十年
我的时代在背后
突然敲响大鼓

POST

An elk heading for the pit-trap
power, the fir tree said, struggle

cherishing the same secret
my hair turned white
retiring, going backward
leaving my post

only one step back
no, ten whole years
my era behind me
suddenly beating on a bass drum

战 后

从梦里蒸馏的形象
在天边遗弃旗帜

池塘变得明亮
那失踪者的笑声
表明：疼痛
是莲花的叫喊

我们的沉默
变成草浆变成
纸，那愈合
书写伤口的冬天

POSTWAR

Images distilled from the dream
abandon the flag at the horizon

the light cast by the pond
the laughter of those missing
makes it clear: pain
is the cry of the lotus

our silence
became straw pulp became
paper, that winter
healing the written wounds

嗅觉

那气味让人记忆犹新
像一辆马车穿过旧货市场
古董、假货和叫卖者的
智慧蒙上了灰尘

和你的现实总有距离
在和老板的争吵中
你看见窗户里的广告
明天多好，明天牌牙膏

你面对着五个土豆
第六个是洋葱
这盘棋的结局如悲伤
从航海图上消失

SMELLS

Those smells making you remember again
like a horse cart passing through the flea market
curios, fakes, hawkers'
wisdom covered in dust

and there's always a gap between you and reality
arguing with the boss
you see the ad out the window
a bright tomorrow, Tomorrow brand toothpaste

you are facing five potatoes
the sixth is an onion
the outcome of this chess game is like sorrow
disappearing from the maritime chart

无 题

被笔勾掉的山水
在这里重现

我指的绝不是修辞
修辞之上的十月
飞行处处可见
黑衣侦察兵
上升，把世界
微缩成一声叫喊

财富变成洪水
闪光一瞬扩展成
过冬的经验
当我像个伪证人
坐在田野中间
大雪部队卸掉伪装
变成语言

UNTITLED

The landscape crossed out with a pen
reappears here

what I am pointing to is not rhetoric
October over the rhetoric
flight seen everywhere
the scout in the black uniform
gets up, takes hold of the world
and microfilms it into a scream

wealth turns into floodwaters
a flash of light expands
into frozen experience
and just as I seem to be a false witness
sitting in the middle of a field
the snow troops remove their disguises
and turn into language

不

答案很快就能知道
日历，那撒谎的光芒
已折射在他脸上

临近遗忘临近
田野的旁白
临近祖国这个词
所拥有的绝望

麦粒饱满
哦成熟的哭泣
今夜最忠实的孤独
在为他引路

他对所有排队
而喋喋不休的日子
说不

NO

The solution soon knows
the calendar, that lying radiance
already refracted in his face

close to forgetting close to
the monologues of open country
close to the homeland this word
all the despair it holds

fat grains of wheat
weep as they ripen
tonight faithful solitude
leads his way

and to all the days in line
endlessly chattering
he says No

中秋节

含果核的情人
许愿，互相愉悦
直到从水下
潜望父母的婴儿
诞生

那不速之客敲我的
门，带着深入
事物内部的决心

树在鼓掌

喂，请等等，满月
和计划让我烦恼
我的手翻飞在
含义不明的信上
让我在黑暗里
多坐一会儿，好像
坐在朋友的心中

这城市如冰海上
燃烧的甲板
得救？是的，得救
水龙头一滴一滴
哀悼着源泉

MOON FESTIVAL

Lovers holding pits in their mouths
make vows and delight in each other
till the underwater infant
periscopes his parents
and is born

an uninvited guest knocks at my
door, determined to go deep
into the interior of things

the trees applaud

wait a minute, the full moon
and this plan are making me nervous
my hand fluttering
over the obscure implications of the letter
let me sit in the dark
a while longer, like
sitting on a friend's heart

the city a burning deck
on the frozen sea
can it be saved? it must be saved
the faucet drip-drop drip-drop
mourns the reservoir

夜 空

沉默的晚餐
盘子运转着黑暗
让我们分享
这煮熟的愤怒
再来点盐

假设拥有更大的
空间——舞台
饥饿的观众
越过我们的表演
目光向上

如升旗，升向
夜空：关闭的广场
一道光芒指出变化
移动行星
我们开始说话

NIGHT SKY

Silent dinner
the dishes spin darkness
letting us share this
simmered anger
add a little salt

suppose there were an even greater
space—a stage
the starving spectators
looking up
at our acting

like raising a flag, rising into
the night sky: the square is shut down
a ray of light points out the changes
shifting planets
we begin to speak

无 题

被雾打湿
念头像被寒流
抖落的鸟群
你必忍受年龄
守望田野
倾听伟大音乐中
迂回的小径

而你是否会被
演奏所忽略
荒芜啊

不，简单
而并不多余
那赞美
那天空与大地
在水面之吻

UNTITLED

Soaked by fog
thoughts like a flock of birds
shake out of the cold drafts
you must endure aging
watch over the fields
listen closely to the circuitous paths
through powerful music

perhaps you were ignored
by the orchestra
desolation

no, simply
not at all superfluously
that praise
that kiss on the water's surface
between sky and earth

出门

罗盘幽默地
指出一种心境
你喝汤然后走出
这生活的场景

天空与电线的
表格上，一棵树
激动得欲飞
又能写些什么

无论如何，你将
重新认识危险
一群陌生人坐在
旅行的终点

风在夜里盗铃
长发新娘
像弓弦起伏在
那新郎身上

LEAVING HOME

The compass jokingly
points toward a state of mind
you drink up the soup and leave
this scene of life

on the application form of
sky and electric wires, a tree
trembling to fly
so what can it write about?

no matter what happens, you'll
recognize the danger
a crowd of strangers sitting
at journey's end

at night the wind steals bells
the long-haired bride
quivers like a bowstring
over the body of the groom

一所尚未放学的学校
暴躁不安但克制
我睡在它旁边
我的呼吸够到课本
新的一课：飞行

当陌生人的骄傲
降下三月雪
树扎根于天空
笔在纸上突围
河的拒绝桥的邀请

上钩的月亮
在我熟悉的楼梯
拐角，花粉与病毒
伤及我的肺伤及
一只闹钟

放学是场革命
孩子们跨越光的栅栏
转入地下
我和那些父母一起
看上升的星星

TEACHER'S MANUAL

A school still in session
irritable restless but exercising restraint
I sleep beside it
my breath just reaching the next
lesson in the textbook: how to fly

when the arrogance of strangers
sends down March snow
a tree takes root in the sky
a pen to paper breaks the siege
the river declines the bridge invites

the moon takes the bait
turning the familiar corner
of the stairs, pollen and viruses
damage my lungs damage
an alarm clock

to be let out of school is a revolution
kids jump over the railings of light
and turn to the underground
other parents and I
watch the stars rise

练习曲

风，树林的穷亲戚
去天边度假
向巨钟滚动的河
投掷柠檬

摄影机追随着阳光
像钢琴调音
那些小小的死亡
音色纯正

写作与战争同时进行
中间建造了房子
人们坐在里面
像谣言，准备出发

戒烟其实是戒掉
一种手势
为什么不说
词还没被照亮

ÉTUDE

Wind, the poor relation of the woods
goes to the horizon to spend its vacation
throwing lemons
into a river rolling with enormous bells

the camera follows the sunlight
like a piano being tuned
those little deaths
pure tone color

war and writing move onward
houses are built between them
people sit there like rumors
waiting to start out

to quit smoking is only to give up
a kind of hand gesture
why not say
words still have not been lit?

怀念

从呼吸困难的
终点转身——
山冈上的落叶天使
屋脊起伏的大海

回到叙述途中
水下梦想的潜水员
仰望飞逝的船只
旋涡中的蓝天

我们讲的故事
暴露了内心的弱点
像祖国之子
暴露在开阔地上

风与树在对话
那一瘸一拐的行走
我们围拢一壶茶
老年

IN MEMORY

Turning back from the end
when it was hard to breathe—
the angels of fallen leaves on the hill
the sea of heaving rooftops

on the way back to the story
the deep-sea diver in the dream
looks up at the ships passing by
blue sky in the whirlpools

the tale we are telling
exposes the weakness in our hearts
like the sons of the nation
laid out on the open ground

dialogue of wind and trees
a limp
we crowd around a pot of tea
old age

晨 歌

词是歌中的毒药

在追踪歌的夜路上
警笛回味着
梦游者的酒精

醒来时头疼
像窗户透明的音箱
从沉默到轰鸣

学会虚度一生
我在鸟声中飞翔
高叫永不

当风暴加满汽油
光芒抓住发出的信
展开，再撕碎

MORNING SONG

Words are the poison in a song

on the track of the song's night road
police sirens   aftertaste
the alcohol of sleepwalkers

waking up, a headache
like the window's transparent speakers
from silence to a roar

learning to waste a lifetime
I hover in the birdcalls
crying never

when the storms have filled up with gas
light rays snatch the letter
unfold it and tear it up

变 形

我背对窗外田野
保持着生活的重心
而五月的疑问
如暴力影片的观众
被烈酒照亮

除了五点钟的蜜
早上的情人正老去
他们合为一体
哦乡愁大海上的
指南针

写作与桌子
有敌意的对角线
星期五在冒烟
有人沿着梯子爬出
观众的视野

DEFORMATION

My back to the window of open fields
holding on to the gravity of life
and the doubts of May
like the audience at a violent movie
lit by drink

except for the honeydrop at five o'clock
the morning's lovers grow old
and become a single body
a compass needle
on a homesick sea

between writing and the table
a diagonal enemy line
Friday in the billowing smoke
someone climbs a ladder
out of sight from the audience

回家

回家，当妄想
收回它的一缕青烟
我的道路平等于
老鼠的隐私

往事令我不安
它是闪电的音叉
伏击那遗忘之手的
隐秘乐器

而此刻的压力
来自更深的蓝色
拐过街角我查看
天书和海的印刷术

我看见我回家
穿过那些夜的玩具
在光的终点
酒杯与呼喊重合

GOING HOME

Going home, useless hope
takes back its wisp of smoke
my road runs parallel
to the privacy of a mouse

the past makes me anxious
it is a tuning fork of lightning
that hidden instrument
trapping a forgotten hand

yet the pressure of this moment
comes from a deeper blue
turning the corner I examine
heaven's book and the printing of the sea

I watch myself going home
passing those nighttime toys
where brightness ends
shouting and wine glasses coincide

狩 猎

女教师早已褪色
却在残缺的日记中
穿针引线
沿不断开方的走廊
全班追赶着兔子
谁剥下它的皮?

后门通向夏天
橡皮永远擦不掉
转变成阳光的虚线
兔子灵魂低飞
寻找投胎人

这是个故事,很多年
有人竖着耳朵

偷看了一眼天空
我们,吮吸红灯的狼
已长大成人

THE HUNT

The teacher faded long ago
yet the fragments of her diary
act as a go-between
following the corridors of continual evolution
the whole team chases the rabbit
who will skin it?

the back door leads to summer
the eraser can never erase
the dotted lines turning into sunlight
the rabbit's soul flies low
looking for its next incarnation

this is a story, many years ago
someone's ears pricked up

stole a glimpse of the sky
and we the wolves suckling on a red lamp
have already grown up

使 命

牧师在祷告中迷路
一扇通风窗
开向另一个时代：
逃亡者在翻墙

气喘吁吁的词在引发
作者的心脏病
深呼吸，更深些
抓住和北风辩论的
槐树的根

夏天到来了
树冠是地下告密者
低语是被蜂群蜇伤的
红色睡眠
不，一场风暴

读者们纷纷爬上岸

MISSION

The priest gets lost in prayer
an air shaft
leads to another era:
escapees climb over the wall

panting words evoke
the author's heart trouble
breathe deep, deeper
grab the locust tree roots
that debate the north wind

summer has arrived
the treetop is an informer
murmurs are a reddish sleep
stung by a swarm of bees
no, a storm

readers one by one clamber onto the shore

转椅

我走出房间
像八音盒里的阴影
太阳的马臀摇晃
在正午站稳

转椅空空
从写作漏斗中
有人被白纸过滤：
一张褶皱的脸
险恶的词

关于忍受自由
关于借光

心，好像用于照明
更多的盲人
往返于昼夜间

SWIVEL CHAIR

I walk out of a room
like a shadow from a music box
the rump of the sun sways
stopping dead at noon

empty empty swivel chair
in the funnel of writing
someone filters through the white paper:
wrinkled face
sinister words

in regard to enduring freedom
in regard to can I have a light

the heart, as if illuminating
even more of the blind
shuttles between day and night

开锁

我梦见我在喝酒
杯子是空的

有人在公园读报
谁说服他到老到天边
吞下光芒？
灯笼在死者的夜校
变成清凉的茶

当记忆斜坡通向
夜空，人们泪水浑浊
说谎——在关键词义
滑向刽子手一边

滑向我：空房子

一扇窗户打开
像高音C穿透沉默
大地与罗盘转动
对着密码——
破晓！

UNLOCK

I dreamt I was drinking wine
the glass was empty

someone reads a newspaper in the park
who persuades him in old age
to swallow light on the horizon?
the lamps at the night school of the dead
turn into cold tea

as the slopes of memory lead
to the night sky, tears turn muddy
people tell lies—at the crux of meaning
they slip alongside the executioner

slip alongside of me: empty house

a window opens
like a high C piercing the silence
earth and compass spin
through the secret combination—
daybreak!

旱季

最初是故乡的风
父亲如飞鸟
在睡意朦胧的河上
突然转向
而你已沉入雾中

如果记忆醒着
像天文台里的夜空
你剪掉指甲
关门开门
朋友难以辨认

直到往日的书信
全部失去阴影
你在落日时分倾听
一个新城市
在四重奏中建成

DRY SEASON

First it's the wind from home
the father like a bird flying
over a river of drowsy haze
suddenly changes course
but you're already sunk in the fog

supposing memory wakes
like the night sky in an observatory
you clip your fingernails
close the door open the door
friends are hard to recognize

until letters from the old days
completely lose their shadows
at sunset you listen closely
to a new city
built by a string quartet

护城河

河水在我心中延伸
又多少燕子
如谦卑的学者加入
这天地间？

一排椅子
开始夜的旅行
我逃学
从十二个时辰
卸下磨盘

如今我老了
像柳树沉入梦中
城门为了遗忘
永远敞开

苹果镀金
女人不再恋爱
词是诱饵
云中伟大的死者
在垂钓我们

MOAT

River stretching in my heart
how many swallows
like modest scholars link
sky and earth?

a row of chairs
starts out on its night journey
I cut class
to unload millstones
from the hours of the day

old now
I'm like a willow sinking into dreams
the city gate opens
to forget

a gilded apple
women will never love again
words are bait
up in the clouds the illustrious dead
fish for us

THE ROSE OF TIME: NEW POEMS
translated by Eliot Weinberger

旅行日记

火车进入森林前
灭火器中的暴风雪睡了
你向过去倾听——

灯光照亮的工地：
手术中剖开的心脏
有人叮当打铁
多么微弱的心跳

桥纵身一跃
把新闻最阴暗的向度
带给明天的城市

前进！深入明天
孩子的语病
和星空的盲文
他们高举青春的白旗
攻占那岁月高地

在终点你成为父亲
大步走过田野
山峰一夜白了头

道路转身

TRAVEL DIARY

before the train enters the forest
a snowstorm in the fire extinguisher falls asleep
you listen to the past—

a construction site lit up:
entrails exposed in surgery
someone hammering bam bam
how weak the heartbeat

a bridge makes a leap
bringing the darkest dimension of the news
to the city of tomorrow

Forward! go deep into the tomorrow
of the kids' awkward wording
and the braille of the starry skies
they hold up the white flag of youth
taking the heights of years by storm

in the end you become a father
striding across the fields
the mountains become white overnight

the road turns back

黑色地图

寒鸦终于拼凑成
夜：黑色地图
我回来了——归程
总是比迷途长
长于一生

带上冬天的心
当泉水和蜜制药丸
成了夜的话语
当记忆狂吠
彩虹在黑市出没

父亲生命之火如豆
我是他的回声
为赴约转过街角
旧日情人隐身风中
和信一起旋转

北京，让我
跟你所有灯光干杯
让我的白发领路
穿过黑色地图
如风暴领你起飞

我排队排到那小窗
关上：哦明月
我回来了——重逢
总是比告别少
只少一次

BLACK MAP

in the end, cold crows piece together
the night: a black map
I've come home—the way back
longer than the wrong road
long as a life

bring the heart of winter
when spring water and horse pills
become the words of night
when memory barks
a rainbow haunts the black market

my father's life-spark small as a pea
I am his echo
turning the corner of encounters
a former lover hides in a wind
swirling with letters

Beijing, let me
toast your lamplights
let my white hair lead
the way through the black map
as though a storm were taking you to fly

I wait in line until the small window
shuts: O the bright moon
I go home—reunions
are one less
fewer than goodbyes

拉姆安拉

在拉姆安拉
古人在星空对弈
残局忽明忽暗
那被钟关住的鸟
跳出来报时

在拉姆安拉
太阳像老头翻墙
穿过露天市场
在生锈的铜盘上
照亮了自己

在拉姆安拉
诸神从瓦罐饮水
弓向独弦问路
一个少年到天边
去继承大海

在拉姆安拉
死亡沿正午播种
在我窗前开花
抗拒之树呈飓风
那狂暴原形

RAMALLAH

in Ramallah
the ancients play chess in the starry sky
the endgame flickers
a bird locked in a clock
jumps out to tell the time

in Ramallah
the sun climbs over the wall like an old man
and goes through the market
throwing mirror light on
a rusted copper plate

in Ramallah
gods drink water from earthen jars
a bow asks a string for directions
a boy sets out to inherit the ocean
from the edge of the sky

in Ramallah
seeds sown along the high noon
death blossoms outside my window
resisting, the tree takes on a hurricane's
violent original shape

盐
——为郎静山《盐厂》题照

底片上暗夜的煤
变成人们每日的盐
一只鸟获得新的高度:
那些屋顶的补丁
让大地更完美

烟高于树
正来自根的记忆
模仿着大雪
时间展示它的富足
从呼喊的盲井
溢出早晨的悲哀

沿东倒西歪的篱笆
风醉倒在路旁
那穿透迷雾的钟声——
让这纸怦然心动

SALT

after the photograph Saltworks *by Chin-San Long*

on the negative   dark night's coal
turns into the people's daily salt
a bird attains new heights
patches of roofs
make the earth more perfect

smoke higher than the trees
it comes from the memory of roots
imitating a heavy snow
time displays its affluence
the blind wells of calling
spill over with morning's sorrow

along the wobbling fence
the drunk wind falls on the roadside
the bell tolling through the mist—
leaves the heart of the paper pounding

给父亲

在二月寒冷的早晨
橡树终有悲哀的尺寸
父亲，在你照片前
八面风保持圆桌的平静

我从童年的方向
看到的永远是你的背影
沿着通向君主的道路
你放牧乌云和羊群

雄辩的风带来洪水
胡同的逻辑深入人心
你召唤我成为儿子
我追随你成为父亲

掌中奔流的命运
带动日月星辰运转
在男性的孤灯下
万物阴影成双

时针兄弟的斗争构成
锐角，合二为一
病雷滚进夜的医院
砸响了你的门

黎明如丑角登场
火焰为你更换床单
钟表停止之处
时间的飞镖呼啸而过

快追上那辆死亡马车吧
一条春天窃贼的小路
查访群山的财富
河流环绕歌的忧伤

TO MY FATHER

on a cold February morning
oaks in the end are the size of sadness
father, in front of your photo
the eight-fold wind keeps the round table calm

from the direction of childhood
I always saw your back
as you herded black clouds and sheep
along the road to emperors

an eloquent wind brings floods
the logic of the alleyways runs deep in the hearts of the people
you sending for me become the son
I following you become the father

fate coursing on the palm of a hand
moves the sun the moon the stars to revolve
beneath a single male lamp
everything has double shadows

the clockhand brothers contend to form
an acute angle, then become one
sick thunder rolls into the hospital of night
pounding on your door

dawn comes up like a clown
flames change the bedsheets for you
where the clock stops
time's dart whistles by

let's catch up to that death-carriage
spring path, a thief
explores for treasure in the mountains
a river circles the song's grief

标语隐藏在墙上
这世界并没多少改变：
女人转身融入夜晚
从早晨走出男人

slogans hide on walls
this world doesn't change much:
a woman turns around blending into night
in the morning a man walks out

那最初的

日夜告别于大树顶端
翅膀收拢最后光芒
在窝藏青春的浪里行船
死亡转动内心罗盘

记忆暴君在时间的
镜框外敲钟——乡愁
搜寻风暴的警察
因辨认光的指纹晕眩

天空在池塘养伤
星星在夜剧场订座
孤儿带领盲目的颂歌
在隘口迎接月亮

那最初的没有名字
河流更新时刻表
太阳撑开它耀眼的伞
为异乡人送行

THE PRIMAL

day and night part at the top of a huge tree
wings close   last light
a boat sails on waves harboring youth
death moves the heart's compass

out of time's frame the tyrant of memory
rings a bell—nostalgia
the policeman searching for a storm
becomes dizzy from identifying the fingerprints of light

the sky heals its wounds in a pond
stars reserve seats at the night's theater
an orphan leads the blind ode
greeting the moon in a mountain pass

the primal has no name
a river updates the schedule
the sun opens its dazzling umbrella
for a stranger starting off

晴 空

夜马踏着路灯驰过
遍地都是悲声
我坐在世纪拐角
一杯热咖啡：体育场
足球比赛在进行
观众跃起变成乌鸦

失败的谣言啊
就像早上的太阳

老去如登高
带我更上一层楼
云中圣者擂鼓
渔船缝纫大海
请沿地平线折叠此刻
让玉米星星在一起

上帝绝望的双臂
在表盘转动

CLEAR SKY

the night horse gallops streetlamps
everywhere the sad sound
I sit at the corner of the centuries
cup of coffee: a stadium
a soccer match going on
fans jumping up like crows

rumors of failure
like the morning sun

aging   an ascent
brings me to a higher floor
sages in the clouds beat drums
a fishing boat sews the sea
please fold this moment at the horizon
let corn and stars come together

the desperate arms of God
move on the clock's face

同 行

这书很重，像锚
沉向生还者的阐释中
你的脸像大洋彼岸的钟
不可能交谈
词整夜在海上漂浮
早上突然起飞

笑声落进空碗里
太阳在肉铺铁钩上转动
头班公共汽车开往
田野尽头的邮局
哦那绿色变奏中的
离别之王

闪电，风暴的邮差
迷失在开花的日子以外
我形影不离紧跟你
从教室走向操场
在迅猛生长的杨树下
变小，各奔东西

COLLEAGUE

this book, heavy as an anchor
sinks among the interpretations of the survivors
your face like a clock on the ocean's far shore
conversation is impossible
words that floated on the sea all night
suddenly take off in the morning

laughter falls into an empty bowl
the sun moves on a butcher's hook
the first scheduled bus goes
to the post office at the end of the fields
in the variations of green
the King of Farewell

lightning, the postman of the storm
gets lost beyond the flowering days
I follow you like a shadow
from the classroom to the playground
under rapidly growing poplars
becoming smaller, each goes his own way

过渡时期

从大海深处归来的人
带来日出的密码
千万匹马被染蓝的寂静

钟这时代的耳朵
因聋而处于喧嚣的中心
苍鹰翻飞有如哑语

为一个古老的口信
虹贯穿所有朝代到此刻
通了电的影子站起来

来自天上细瘦的河
穿过小贩初恋的枣树林
晚霞正从他脸上消失

汉字印满了暗夜
电视上刚果河的鳄鱼
咬住做梦人的膀胱

当筷子拉开满月之弓
厨师一刀斩下
公鸡脑袋里的黎明

TRANSITIONAL PERIOD

from deep sea someone comes
bringing the sunrise code
the silence of thousands of dying horses in the blue

a deaf bell, ear of the era,
is at the center of noise,
hawk flies: sign language

delivering an ancient message
the rainbow crosses all the dynasties to this moment
electrified shadows stand up

a slender river from heaven cuts through
the jujube forests of a street vendor's first love
the sunset glow vanishes from his face

Chinese characters are printed over the dark night
a crocodile in the Congo River on TV
bites into the bladder of a dreamer

chopsticks pulled on the bow of a full moon
with one whack the cook chops off
the dawn in the chicken's head

读 史

梅花暴动中敌意的露水
守护正午之剑所刻下的黑暗
革命始于第二天早晨
寡妇之怨像狼群穿过冻原

祖先们因预言而退入
那条信仰与欲望激辩的河流
没有尽头，只有漩涡隐士
体验另一种冥想的寂静

登高看王位上的日落
当文明与笛声在空谷飘散
季节在废墟上站起
果实翻过墙头追赶明天

READING HISTORY

hostile dew in an uprising of plum blossoms
guards the darkness etched by the noon sword
a revolution begins the following morning
the bitterness of the widows cuts through the tundra like a pack of
wolves

on account of the prophecies the ancestors are moving backward
into that river of the furious debates of faith and desire
that never end, only a hermit swirl
learns another silence of meditation

go up to see the sunset of kingship
when civilization and flute songs float off in an empty valley
the seasons stand up in the ruins
fruits climb over the walls to chase tomorrow

致 敬
　　　——给G.艾基（Gennady Aygi）

大雪剪纸中的细节
火光深处的城市——
绕过垂钓梦者的星星
行船至急转弯处
你用词语压舱

母亲的歌传遍四方

水壶中的风暴尖叫——
家园正驶离站台
打开你的窗户
此刻带领以往的日子
如大雁南飞

田野，你的悲伤

你排队买煤油
和人们跃入黑暗
带喉音的时代在呼喊：
也许是命运也许是
小号的孤独

哦嘹亮的时刻

俄罗斯母亲
是你笔下奔流的长夜
覆盖墓地的大雪
那等待砍伐的森林
有斧子的忧郁

TRIBUTE
  to Gennady Aygi

intricacies of paper-cuts of snow
the city in deep flame—
around the stars fishing for dreamers
you sail the sharp bend of the river
you ballast words

songs of the Mother spread everywhere

a storm screams in a kettle—
the homeland is leaving from the platform
open your window
this moment leads the days of the past
like wild geese heading south

the field, your sadness

on the queue for kerosene
you jump into the darkness with the others
the guttural age cries out:
perhaps it is destiny perhaps
the isolation of a trumpet

moment resonant

Mother Russia
a long night flowing from your pen
a heavy snow covering the cemeteries
the forest waits to be logged
as melancholic as the ax

青 灯
  ——给魏斐德

故国残月
沉入深潭中
重如那些石头
你把词语垒进历史
让河道转弯

花开几度
催动朝代盛衰
乌鸦即鼓声
帝王们如蚕吐丝
为你织成长卷

美女如云
护送内心航程
青灯掀开梦的一角
你顺手挽住火焰
化作漫天大雪

把酒临风
你和中国一起老去
长廊贯穿春秋
大门口的陌生人
正砸响门环

THE GREEN LAMP
for Fred Wakeman

old country   waning moon
sinking in a deep pond
heavy as those stones
words you lay into history
let the course of the river bend

how many blossoms
drive the rise and fall of dynasties
the crows are the drumbeats
emperors like silkworms spin
weaving a long scroll for you

the legendary beauties like clouds
escort the voyages in the heart
a green lamp lifts a corner of the dream
you curl into a flame
that turns into heavy snow

holding wine in the wind
aging with China
a long corridor cuts through springs and autumns
strangers at the gate
are pounding on the knocker

路 歌

在树与树的遗忘中
是狗的抒情进攻
在无端旅途的终点
夜转动所有的金钥匙
没有门开向你

一只灯笼遵循的是
冬天古老的法则
我径直走向你
你展开的历史折扇
合上是孤独的歌

晚钟悠然追问你
回声两度为你作答
暗夜逆流而上
树根在秘密发电
你的果园亮了

我径直走向你
带领所有他乡之路
当火焰试穿大雪
日落封存帝国
大地之书翻到此刻

ROAD SONG

in the oblivion between the trees
the lyric attacks by dogs
at the end of an endless trip
night turns all the keys of gold
but no door opens for you

a lantern follows
the ancient principles of winter
I walk straight toward you
as you open the fan of history
that's folded in an isolated song

the evening bell slowly questions you
echoes answer for you twice
dark night sails against the current
tree roots secretly generating electricity
have lit your orchard

I walk straight toward you
at the head of all the foreign roads
when fire tries on the heavy snow
sunset seals the empire
the earth's book turns the page of this moment

过冬

醒来：北方的松林——
大地紧迫的鼓声
树干中阳光的烈酒
激荡黑暗之冰
而心与狼群对喊

风偷走的是风
冬天因大雪的债务
大于它的隐喻
乡愁如亡国之君
寻找的是永远的迷失

大海为生者悲亡
星星轮流照亮爱情——
谁是全景证人
引领号角的河流
果园的暴动

听见了吗？我的爱人
让我们手挽手老去
和词语一起冬眠
重织的时光留下死结
或未完成的诗

PASSING WINTER

waking: forest in the north
urgent drumbeats on the earth
sunlight's hard liquor in the tree trunks
agitates the ice of darkness
the heart cries out with a pack of wolves

what the wind steals is wind
winter with a deficit of snow
is bigger than its metaphor
the homesick like a king who's lost his country
seek what is gone forever

the ocean mourns for all the living
the stars take turns illuminating love
Who is the witness of the panorama
leading a river from the brass horns
and the riots of an orchard?

Have you heard? my love
let's get old together holding hands
hibernating with words
in the reweaving of time some knots remain
or an unfinished poem

时间的玫瑰

当守门人沉睡
你和风暴一起转身
拥抱中老去的是
时间的玫瑰

当鸟路界定天空
你回望那落日
消失中呈现的是
时间的玫瑰

当刀在水中折弯
你踏笛声过桥
密谋中哭喊的是
时间的玫瑰

当笔画出地平线
你被东方之锣惊醒
回声中开放的是
时间的玫瑰

镜中永远是此刻
此刻通向重生之门
那门开向大海
时间的玫瑰

THE ROSE OF TIME

when the watchman falls asleep
you turn back with the storm
to grow old embracing is
the rose of time

when bird roads define the sky
you look behind at the sunset
to emerge in disappearance is
the rose of time

when the knife is bent in water
you cross the bridge stepping on flute-songs
to cry in the conspiracy is
the rose of time

when a pen draws the horizon
you're awakened by a gong from the East
to bloom in the echoes is
the rose of time

in the mirror there is always this moment
this moment leads to the door of rebirth
the door opens to the sea
the rose of time

Zhao Zhenkai was born in Beijing in 1949, less than two months
before the birth of the People's Republic of China. From a formerly
aristocratic and later middle-class family, he received an elite educa-
tion until the Cultural Revolution closed down the schools in 1966.
He was sent into the countryside and worked for eleven years as a
concrete mixer building roads and bridges and as a blacksmith.

Back in Beijing in the late 1970s, he and a group of young poets be-
gan writing in a way that was a conscious rejection of the folkloric
and socialist realist literature that had been required by Mao Zedong
since his famous speech in Yenan in 1942. (Though Mao, who wrote
classical poems, made an exception for himself.) Their models were
the translations written by an older generation of Chinese modern-
ists who were not allowed to publish their own work, but who could
translate poets with the proper political credentials—such as Lorca,
Neruda, Alberti, Eluard, and Aragon—even though this work was
radically different from officially accepted content and form. Curi-
ously, and quite coincidentally, many of these same European and
Latin American poets were, at this same moment, important influ-
ences on a new generation of American poets.

The young poets gave each other pseudonyms, as was common in
the Chinese tradition. Zhao Zhenkai was called Bei Dao ("North
Island") because he came from the north and his temperament was
that of solitude. The poetry they wrote was imagistic, subjective, and
often surreal. Although it had no overt political content, its assertion
of individual sentiments and perceptions, of imagination itself, was
considered subversive in a collectivist society. In 1978, their work be-
came a kind of poetic conscience for the student demonstrators of
the Democracy Movement. Bei Dao's "The Answer" with its simple
and impassioned line, "I—do—not—believe!" was the movement's
"Blowin' in the Wind," and it was reproduced on countless wall
posters. The poets became pop stars, read to stadiums full of fans,
and were chased down the street in scenes out of *A Hard Day's Night.*

The new poetry, published in China's first samisdat magazine, *Jin-
tian* [*Today*], edited by Bei Dao, was officially denounced during

the so-called Anti-Spiritual Pollution Campaign as *menglong*. (The word literally means "misty," but it does not have the same saccharine connotations in Chinese as it does in English: "obscure" or "vague" would be more exact.) *Jintian* was effectively shut down, but the young poets ironically and enthusiastically embraced *menglong* as the name for their movement.

"Obscure"—or, as it was known in the West, "Misty"—poetry would remain the primary expression for the change of consciousness yearned for by the next generation of student demonstrators, those who occupied Tiananmen Square in 1989. I recall an interview with Wuer Kaixi, one of the student leaders, some months after the government massacre that ended the protest movement and sent many into prison and exile. Wuer, a largely uneducated peasant from the far west of China who had been given a scholarship to attend Beijing University, was asked where he had found his political ideas. He replied, "I got them from reading the poetry of Bei Dao."

Bei Dao himself happened to be in Europe giving readings at the time of the massacre. He knew that he could not return, and he has been in exile ever since, for many years in various countries of northern Europe (where, as he wrote, he had to speak Chinese to the mirror) and then in the United States. He supported himself by writing regular columns for Taiwanese newspapers, short-term residencies at remote colleges, and by giving readings around the world. For the first seven of those years, his wife and young daughter were not allowed to leave China, and he never saw them.

As is common with poets who became famous young, the appreciation of his work often seems to remain frozen in the early writing. But— as will be obvious from this selection spanning thirty years—Bei Dao is not the same poet that he was in his "obscure" days. His work has grown increasingly complex, partially owing to his discovery, in exile, of the poetries of Paul Celan and César Vallejo, who have become his kindred spirits, along with Osip Mandelstam, the Chuvash poet Gennadi Aygi, Tomas Tranströmer, and, unexpectedly, Dylan Thomas.

In 1990, *Jintian* was revived as a forum for the Chinese diaspora, and it continues under Bei Dao's editorial direction. At this writing, while most of the other exiled writers have been given permission to visit or return, Bei Dao is still barred from entering China. Recently his books have been allowed to be published on the mainland, where they have become best sellers, and, somewhat surprisingly, he has been permitted to teach in Hong Kong, where he currently lives with his second wife, the editor and publisher Gan Qi, and their son.

ELIOT WEINBERGER
September 2009

INDEX OF TITLES AND FIRST LINES